# WALKING IN AWE

## Musings of a Nature-Loving Nonprofit Director

*Dave Van Manen* (signature)

**Dave Van Manen**

**Walking in Awe: Musings of a Nature-Loving Nonprofit Director**
© 2023, David Van Manen

Books may be purchased in quantity and/or special sales by contacting the publisher. All inquiries related to such matters should be addressed to:

Middle Creek Publishing & Audio
9161 Pueblo Mountain Park Road
Beulah, CO 81023

editor@middlecreekpublishing.com

(719) 369-9050

First Paperback Edition, 2023

ISBN: 978-1-957483-12-2

Front Cover Image: Helene Van Manen
Back cover image: Dave Van Manen
Interior illustrations: Scarlett Stulb
Author Image: Helene Van Manen

Printed in the United States

# WALKING IN AWE

## Musings of a Nature-Loving Nonprofit Director

**Dave Van Manen**

**Illustrations by Scarlett Stulb**

**Middle Creek Publishing & Audio**
**Beulah, CO    USA**

*Dedicated to my grandchildren, Jude and Scarlett.*

# Contents

## Preface

I've always had a love for Nature. It began when I was a child in the tiny backyard of my New York City home and the summer woods, beaches and bays on Long Island. When I moved to a little town in Colorado's southern foothills at the age of 20, my love for Nature grew exponentially. For nearly five decades, the town of Beulah has been my home. Moving from a bustling metropolis with over fifteen million people to a tiny mountain hamlet with a population of less than a thousand suited me just fine. I often said that when I lived in New York City I felt like a fish out of water.

Living in Beulah, on the eastern side of the Wet Mountains at an elevation of around 6500 feet, provided easy access to Nature. Within an hour's drive, I could be hiking in the Sangre de Cristo Wilderness or the Greenhorn Mountain Wilderness. Even closer was the 611-acre Pueblo Mountain Park, a sparsely developed piece of relatively wild land, with six miles of trails that connected the park to thousands of acres of the adjacent San Isabel National Forest. The park's main entrance was, and still is, just a five-minute walk from my funky old cabin home. The view outside my cabin's western windows takes in the entirety of the Mountain Park. I was a serious student of the natural world, and Pueblo Mountain Park was an ideal classroom.

My study of Nature took place alongside raising two children and, as part of a musical duo with my wife Helene, making a living as a musician. "The Van Manens" specialized in Nature-based songs and stories for children. In the late 1990s, we were both ready to move on from the music business. Helene became a business and leadership coach, and I started the nonprofit Mountain Park Environmental Center (MPEC), which officially began operations in February 2000. With a mission focused on Nature education, MPEC's home base was Pueblo Mountain Park.

The Mountain Park is owned by the City of Pueblo and is located around 25 miles west of Pueblo. In the couple of decades leading up to the opening of MPEC, the park was little used for much of each year (notwithstanding it being my Nature classroom); it was even rumored that the City was interested in liquidating the park. The success of MPEC's programs breathed new life into Pueblo Mountain Park and silenced any rumors of the park being sold to some real estate developer.

I served as MPEC's Executive Director for fifteen years or so, after which I stepped down, but continued to serve the organization in various capacities for several more years. In 2018, the organization known as the Mountain Park Environmental Center was retired when it merged with another local nonprofit, and still operates in Pueblo Mountain Park.

## Introduction

Most of the essays in *Walking in Awe,* save for a few exceptions, were written out along the trails of Pueblo Mountain Park, and were originally published in the *Mountain Park News,* the newsletter of the Mountain Park Environmental Center. I believe it was songwriter Paul Simon who said that songs are like snapshots. They capture a particular moment in the life of the songwriter. Simon's analogy can easily be applied to the essays in this book. Written over a couple of decades, each essay captures a moment in my life, or, more precisely, my thoughts. Just as a photographer will capture a certain subject from several angles, many of the essays explore certain themes or topics from several angles. Like the seasons that circle back around every year, many of the same topics circle back to find their way into these essays several times.

Some of the recurring themes include common local species of flora and fauna; the importance and value of Nature education; the weather and the changing seasons; the growing awareness of how quickly time seems to be slipping by and its relationship to my own mortality; the ongoing challenge of managing what often felt like too many things that my job as an Executive Director of a growing nonprofit demanded of me. A project that is referenced in a few essays is the major renovation of the Depression-era Horseshoe Lodge, a project I spearheaded and managed that transformed a tired and neglected structure in the Mountain Park into a vibrant center for Nature education and recreation.

As I was compiling these essays, I noticed that drought was

a topic I wrote about quite often. This was no surprise. Much of the western United States has been in the throes of extreme drought since the year 2000—the year MPEC opened its doors. Often referred to as a megadrought, it is the region's worst dry spell in 1,200 years. Coupled with the fact that my home and workplace are both in what wildland firefighters refer to as "the wildland urban interface," an area where human development and forested wildlands intermingle, it is no wonder that drought was a topic that found its way into several essays.

There has never been a clear line that separates my personal life and my professional life. This has been especially so regarding my love of Nature and my career as MPEC's Executive Director. MPEC itself was born out of my love for the natural world, and the trajectory the organization took was inseparable from my evolving relationship with and understanding of Nature—my growing skills as a Nature educator and naturalist; threats to the Earth's ecological integrity; societal attitudes towards the natural world; those individuals and groups working to protect it. As such, I seldom made much of an effort to separate the personal and the professional as I wrote these essays. In essence, that personal/professional dichotomy hardly existed for me. The essays in *Walking in Awe* offer many glimpses into the struggles, the joys, the values, the passions, the activities, and the thoughts of a person whose time "at work" and time "not at work" often looked and felt very much the same.

The thread that ties together the essays in *Walking in Awe* is my deep love for the natural world, the awe that this love arouses in me, and how walking and hiking have been inseparable from my experience of awe. A life immersed in Nature is a life filled with awe. Of course, it can't be denied that the other side of the coin from awe for the Nature-lover is grief. A lover of the natural world cannot but grieve over the countless wounds inflicted on it by people. Some of the essays give voice to that pain. But mostly, this book is about being in awe—in awe of Nature's unrelenting beauty, her countless mysteries, her grace, her raw power, her wildness, her resilience, her fragility, her amazing expressions of life—and being in awe of the peace, and even the comfort, that comes with knowing that Nature always bats last!

## The Art of Walking
*December 5, 2001*

*November 28: It was a delightful walk over to the Center this morning. Tracks of deer, squirrel, and several foxes (or one well-traveled fox) were slowing down my arrival to work as I found myself closely examining the tracks, and even following them a bit....*

This excerpt from my current journal reveals a theme found throughout my two decades of journal-keeping—walking in Nature. Walking is, in my estimation, one of the true joys of living.

Even as a young person, I used to love walking. Onderdonk Avenue past Grove Street over to Linden Street. Take a left up Linden, past the block where I played stickball and touch football, past Woodward, Fairview and Grandview Avenues, all the way to Fresh Pond Road. In spite of the street names promising nice views and fresh ponds, these were not strolls in the country. My New York City childhood was a city childhood, but it was a life of walking nonetheless.

Henry David Thoreau had a more rural landscape in mind when he wrote, "I have met but one or two persons in the course of my life who understood the art of Walking, that is, of taking walks,—who had a genius, so to speak, for *sauntering…*" Now, thankfully, my walks, like Henry Thoreau's, are more rural. To simply saunter, with no real destination, no plan, just a wanderer in the woods—these are the best walks.

Mr. Thoreau states, "My vicinity affords many good walks." I have been to his vicinity in Massachusetts. I have walked the shores of Walden Pond, and I've sat and journaled at his cabin-site. A great place to walk—though some of the ruralness has been lost to development.

I, too, can state that my vicinity affords many good walks. In fact, the trails and woods of this Mountain Park are a paradise for the walker, the saunterer, the Nature-lover. Rural, relatively wild and undeveloped, accessible. Undeniably, we are all blessed to have this wonderful place to walk, to saunter, to wander, to discover Nature.

I know what Henry David meant when he said, "I think that I cannot preserve my health and spirits, unless I spend four hours a day at least... sauntering through the woods and fields..." My walks in Nature have become much more than recreation, or exercise. So much bad news about bombings, war, starving children, environmental destruction and the like can be genuine threats to my mental health. Truly, walking has become my primary anti-depressant! I'll add that Henry was lucky: four hours. But I do the best that I can.

My Mountain Park walks these days occur in a landscape dominated by muted browns and yellows, ever-greens, and varying amounts of white, depending on the snow. My companions are the many winter birds, who I hear as much as I see, and an assortment of mammals—well, their tracks, anyway. And, of course, my journal.

*November 23: I am sitting under a white fir up on the Mace Trail—snowing strong right now—I just had a great hike up Devil's Canyon. It feels <u>so good</u> to be out on this wintry day....*

## The Mountains are Calling
*February 2, 2002*

> *"The mountains are calling and I must go."*
> *~ John Muir*

I spent most of this last week being one with my computer. I finished up a major grant proposal, and, as Friday afternoon started to hint of Friday evening, major grant proposal number two was underway. As I closed and locked the MPEC door and made my way home in the frosty pink twilight, I vowed to the trees that I would impose a weekend separation between me and my computer. It would do our relationship good, I thought. Dell, goodbye (until Monday).

I woke up this Saturday morning to a gray-and-white kind of day. No bright sun or blue sky—just an overcast sky and a landscape covered by a 2-day-old, 7-inch snow. Perfect weather. You see, I try to adhere to a philosophy articulated by English writer and philosopher John Ruskin, "There is really no such thing as bad weather, only different kinds of good weather." And that snow-covered gray-sky world out there was calling my name. So, now, here I am, perched on a favorite hilltop, tucked under a large Douglas fir tree with my journal and a pair of binoculars ... Dell who?

The hike up here was frequently interrupted by several short tracking detours. Though it seems as if I have this whole park to myself this early morning, that holds true only in human terms. As my detours prove, I am certainly not alone out here—though my park comrades are a shy bunch. Plenty of sign, but not a glimpse of the creatures themselves.

And what creatures, you may be asking? For a long stretch along the trail, I walked side by side with the tracks of a fox. A couple of little patches of yellow snow alongside small clumps of mountain mahogany told me this canine was saying, "This is my territory." "I'm just visiting," I promised. I noticed the delicate tracks of several mice, tails dragging behind, and the clumsy tracks of a few turkeys. Evidence of several deer of various sizes was also obvious. A stretch of faint tracks on some crusty snow had me guessing until a nasal inspection of a small patch of yellow instantly revealed the unmistakable musk of a skunk that must have ventured out overnight.

As the minutes have now become over an hour, and my writing is interspersed with long stretches of just sitting and watching, I've become aware of how profoundly still the park is. Not necessarily quiet, but still. I'm reminded of a passage by Edward Abbey on his first day at his backcountry post at Arches National Monument, "...the air is untroubled, and I become aware for the first time today of the immense silence in which I am lost. Not a silence so much as a stillness—for there are a few sounds: the creak of some bird in a juniper tree, an eddy of wind which passes and fades like a sigh..." The few sounds within this Mountain Park stillness include the *peep* of a Townsend's solitaire, the nasal *yank* of a red-breasted nuthatch, the periodic percussive impacts of tree-borne snow with the ground, and a woodpecker in the distance, hammering away for some breakfast.

Of all the things that call me to the natural world, it is probably the stillness that calls the loudest, and that I love the most. And why I, too, like John Muir, must go!

## I'm Setting My Clock to Nature Time
*April 7, 2002*

It is the morning of Sunday, April 7, and I am tucked against a large rock just south of Lookout Point on this, the first day of daylight-saving time. Of course, no daylight is really being saved, as far as I can tell. By turning our clocks forward, we all just agreed to get up and be at work or school or wherever an hour earlier than last week. I suppose that is somehow more acceptable than telling everyone they must be wherever they need to be at 7 a.m. instead of 8 a.m. for the next seven months or so.

It has always seemed kind of strange to me, this "springing forward and falling back" of our clocks twice a year. I once read a Native American commentary on the time change. It said that the twice-a-year adjustment to our clocks is like cutting a few inches off the end of a blanket in the spring and sewing it on the other end of the blanket. Then, in the fall, you remove the sewn section from that end and sew it back in its original place on the blanket. Doing this year after year after year—it's still the same blanket, and it's still the same size. What's being saved? Amusing, he thought!

From my rocky vantage point, with the walls of the canyon dropping off to my right, I look around at a landscape that couldn't care less about whether it is now 11 a.m. or 10 a.m. These mountains full of trees and wildflowers and shrubs and birds and everything else adhere to a sense of time much more ancient than the human construct of time.

Yesterday's first sighting of a turkey vulture, returning to its summer breeding grounds; the first purple blossoms of larkspur that I just saw, poking through the leaf duff; the swelling buds of the Gambel oak all around me, just a few weeks away from bringing forth some of this season's greenery; the least chipmunks that are again feeding below the bird feeders, awake from their winter dormancy—these all speak of a more primal rhythm to the passage of time, one much slower, drawn out, sane. The orange rocks of this canyon (batholithic granite of Mesozoic Era, according to the books) that go back millions of years make the human preoccupation with time seem, well, even more amusing. And a bit less important.

When my life begins to feel too full of schedules and appointments and seeming like I do not have enough time, this is where I need to bring myself. Places like this help put things back into perspective. There is something about seeing that first turkey vulture or finding that first larkspur bloom that somehow comforts me, somehow brings a touch of sanity to what sometimes feels like, well, insanity. Seeing these things is a reminder that the rhythms of the natural world often make so much more sense than the frenetic world of appointments and schedules that I spend much of my life in.

Are those Pasqueflowers blooming yet? I need to go see!

**Dirty Socks**
*April 11, 2002*

A recent conversation with my 22-year-old daughter, Sierra, put a smile on my face, just as she said it would. She works as a medical assistant at a pediatrician's office in Pueblo. It went something like this:

*Sierra:* Dad, you'll never guess what happened at work today.
*Dave:* You got a big raise?
*S:* No, I had a 10-year-old boy with really dirty socks.
*D:* And that's supposed to make me smile?
*S:* Let me explain. His Mom brought him in for a physical, so I told him to take off his shoes so we could get an accurate height and weight. As he took them off, I noticed his socks were caked with dirt. His Mom also noticed, and rather embarrassed, asked him why he hadn't changed his socks since yesterday. When I asked what happened yesterday, he said, "Oh, my class spent the day up in Beulah for this great field trip at the Mountain Park. I didn't want to change my socks 'cause this is Beulah dirt. That

was the best day of school I ever had." So I asked him if he met Ranger Dave. "Sure, Ranger Dave took us on this really cool hike. We learned about ponderosa pine trees and tassel-eared squirrels and animal tracks. That's how my socks got so dirty—the trail was really muddy. But how do you know about Ranger Dave?" So I told him that you were my Dad! He thought that was really cool!

*D:* Well, I'm smiling now.

*S:* I told you it would make you smile!

Sierra was right. Her sweet little story made my day, and I am still smiling!

## In Love with Nature
*June 1, 2002*

*"We cannot win this battle to save species and environments without forging an emotional bond between ourselves and nature as well—for we will not fight to save what we do not love."*
~ *Stephen Jay Gould*

My morning walk on this hot June day didn't go very far. Tired from a busy week of many guided hikes, hot dry weather, and vanloads of students, I quickly realized that the more distant trails of the western half of the Mountain Park were not going to be a part of this walk. I instead chose to saunter; I would go where the breeze—and the shade—led.

As I approached the small trail that leads from the Horseshoe Lodge to the pond, a quick flying bird caught my attention. I looked up to watch a pretty violet-green swallow land on a branch of a very large ponderosa snag. I know this majestic tree—I've been watching it for years. It is one of the park's older ponderosas, one of the "yellow-barks." It probably started growing around 1850, maybe earlier.

11

This tree has character. Dwarf mistletoe; a long vertical scar from a long-ago lightning strike; significant sections of rot, peppered with holes of various sizes have all left their mark. It also has resiliency, as it didn't succumb to any of these. But when mountain pine beetles hit it a couple of years ago, it had no fight left. It is now a snag.

The tree's many holes have provided nesting habitat for countless birds through many breeding seasons. The swallow I noticed was a male, perched outside an upper cavity. Along with its somewhat less colorful mate, these birds are now tenants of one of the snag's upper cavities. The many smaller holes indicate that more than a few creatures have found some good insect-eating from this tree. Like a multi-story apartment building/supermarket, this tree does and will continue to play an important role in this ponderosa pine ecosystem.

I continued along the trail, gingerly avoided some persistent poison ivy, and am now sitting at the edge of the park's main pond, where these words are being written. I pause often, to look, and listen, remember, and feel. Looking down at the pond, I see the green of inverted pines and the lighter green of Gambel oaks rippling in the water's mirror surface, all against a backdrop of rich blue sky. Water striders add circular patterns that quickly grow themselves away.

I hear a multitude of birds—a black-headed grosbeak singing with abandon; the melancholy call of a mourning dove tugs on childhood memories graced by this sweet sound; the trill of a red-winged blackbird, not very common in the park; a house wren, incessantly stating ownership of its territory above the pond.

This pond and I go way back. If I close my eyes, I can see my first look at an American dipper "swimming" underwater, propelled by its wings; my children, muddy and wet, hunting for snails; bear tracks discovered one fall morning; a kingfisher, patiently waiting for a fishy meal while perched on an overhanging branch; drilling a hole through 12 inches of ice for a cold and boring introduction to ice-fishing.

What do I feel right now? This is as peaceful a moment as I've had in some time. It feels so good to bask in this peacefulness. I also feel an emotional bond with this place, with this park, with the natural world, that could easily be called love. Author and scientist E.O. Wilson calls this feeling *biophilia*—the love of Nature.

There is no need to walk any further. For this morning saunter, I have walked as far as I need to walk. I think I'll just sit here and look, listen, remember, and feel the love!

## Some Deep Thinking after a Green River Float Trip
*August 19, 2002*

I just returned from a fantastic float trip down the Green River in Southeast Utah. Though the water was low, it was still a magical journey full of beautiful landscapes, good friends, and lots of time to just look around and think. I was reminded of how valuable spending time in Nature can be in giving folks a break from the stresses of our busy lives. Seldom did I think about the many challenges I've been dealing with as the director of a Nature education center during these extremely dry months, with tinder-dry forests and the ongoing threat of wildfire. My primary intention for the trip was to relax and flow with the river—and that I did!

My secondary intention was to learn more about the ecology of this section of the Colorado Plateau. With limited first-hand experience in these desert ecosystems, I spent much of my time comparing what I saw to what I am most familiar with—the ecosystems of Pueblo Mountain Park. The similarities were many, but not surprising, as there are many desert-like qualities to the Mountain Park in Beulah.

Where Rocky Mountain junipers are an important food-producing tree here in the park, Utah juniper is the common juniper in the shrublands along the Green River. Both trees produce small cones, or "berries," that feed many species of birds and small mammals in their respective places. This is known as an *ecological equivalent*—different species serving similar ecological roles in different ecosystems. Some of the Utah junipers appeared to be many hundreds of years old, maybe older. I saw almost no Gambel oak, so prevalent here in the park. But I became very familiar with the scraggly leaves of greasewood. The rabbitbrush, some already with bright yellow flowers, reminded me of places around the Greenway and Nature Center in Pueblo.

Along with many great blue herons, a few raptors, and some Canada geese, other frequently spotted birds were sandpipers, flycatchers and cliff swallows (munching on flying insects every evening). Among the mammals seen were desert bighorns, a couple of gigantic beavers, and a herd of wild horses. The fresh mountain lion track and older bear tracks near one night's camp had us overly attentive to every sound that night. I saw only one snake—a very long garter snake—and about a million lizards.

After the rather difficult task of leaving the river—most of us were simply not ready for the wonderful trip to end—we took an hour-long bus ride back to Moab. After a few minutes winding through a hot, treeless, shrubless landscape, we rounded a bend in the road and a lovely view of the river came into full view. I immediately thought, "There's my river." Just as this thought registered, I heard a young girl say to her Dad, "There's our river." Then I heard another voice on the bus say the same thing. Then another. I was struck with what I was hearing. These words

15

indicated the sense of ownership that took place during those five days on this slow-moving murky river. Prior to this trip, the Green River was a squiggly blue line on a map. Now, for me, and, apparently several others, the Green has become something dear to us, something that is a part of us.

After several days thinking about this, I realize, once again, how vitally important it is for people to have opportunities to get to know a landscape – a river, a mountain, a forest, a park – deeply. Knowledge of and connection with the land is the foundation of a sense of ownership and stewardship of that land. And now, I am ready to be back at my work, because this is what we do here at the Mountain Park Environmental Center—provide opportunities for our community to know, connect with, and ultimately become advocates of this park, these ecosystems, these places—our places!

## Hurry, Hurry, Hurry—For What?
*October 8, 2002*

*"We hurry through our meals to go to work and hurry through our work in order to 'recreate' ourselves in the evenings and on weekends and vacations. And then we hurry, with the greatest possible speed and noise and violence, through our recreation—for what?"*
*~ Wendell Berry*

It is going to be a busy workday today. Students will be arriving in an hour and a half, the newsletter needs to be written, there is a quarterly report that needs to be completed and mailed soon…plenty to do. With such thoughts in mind, I walked out my door at home this morning and proceeded right past my car. You see, when the overwhelm hits, as it frequently does, I can easily slip into a *rush to work* mentality, "The sooner I get there, the more I can get done—so, drive the short distance instead of walk." Not today—I managed to get right past the car and I walked to work. A smart start to a busy day, if I say so myself!

The air was cool—pleasantly cool after this terribly hot summer. Yes, summer is over—officially by dates, certainly by the look and feel of the day. One thing I love about autumn is how cool evenings and mornings are juxtaposed against gentle warm days.

There is less sun at 8 a.m. and the light is different—it looks and feels, well, changed. It is softer, kinder, mellower than the summer sun. The day's shadows are longer, as the sun is noticeably lower in the sky than it was in June as summer was getting underway. During this second week of October, three weeks after the autumn equinox, the sun is positioned about the same as during the first week of March—three weeks *before* the *spring* equinox. Of course, in March, I'll write that the sun is noticeably *higher* than it was in December at winter's start, and note that the light is, well, changed. Ah, the reliability of the seasons—such comfort during these times of war and drought and uncertainty.

I walked slowly this morning, not because I dreaded getting to work, but because I wanted to be aware of everything around me. The significant moisture of the last few weeks (3.7 inches since September 8) had produced obvious results. Seeds of all varieties had sprouted into countless green seedlings. Grasses that appeared dead a month ago had apparently been only dormant, holding life in their roots until the rains brought it out. It was like spring, in October. There were a few asters and gumweed in bloom as well.

As I crossed over the creek bed, I noticed several juncos flitting around the still-green willows. A deeply striped brownish sparrow gave me only a split-second opportunity to refine my identification of the quick-moving bird. It was a—sparrow.

As I walked into the park and turned towards the Center where my office awaits, I noticed the many colors that the oaks are wearing. From late-summer green to pretty-much brown, it was the yellows and oranges that lit up the landscape. I heard the squeak of a woodpecker call, and then the rattle of bill against wood. Pine beetles beware!

Just a few hundred feet from the Center, the yellow-leaved chokecherries hung over bright red poison ivy. The thought occurred to me that an unaware person could get quite an unpleasant surprise if they chose to pick some of these colorful, red-leafed plants to brighten up their kitchen tables. Even in fall or winter, the rash-producing urushiol of poison ivy is present and ready to go to work. Picker beware!

In a few hours, I will be taking this same walk in the opposite direction, pleased after a productive day at work, and pleased that I wisely decided to start this day with a slow walk instead of a quick drive. I think I'll walk home slowly too!

## Where I Go to Find Peace
*December 3, 2002*

*"The first fall of snow is not only an event, it is a magical event...if this is not enchantment, then where is it to be found?"*
*~ J.B. Priestley*

The snow began to fall shortly after I arrived at the office this morning. By nine o'clock, the ground's earthy colors were already covered with enough white that the date and the landscape matched rather well. And now, as the light now begins to hint that evening is not far off, I am tucked underneath a healthy white fir tree, protected from most of the falling snow by a roof of needled branches.

I sit absolutely still. I look, and I listen. This tree shelter is located in a deep, trail-less drainage just west of the park's upper road. It is surrounded by a dense forest of Douglas and white firs. The orange bark of a few ponderosa pines adds a bit of color to this world of grays, muted greens and white.

The falling snow is so fine it makes no sound as it settles on the branches and ground. The only sound is the busy work of a woodpecker somewhere up the steep slope to my left. Again, I am perfectly still. Minutes go by with nothing to hear but the woodpecker. Suddenly, the unmistakable heavy pounding of a running ungulate draws my eyes further up the slope. A deer, apparently frightened, bounces through the trees. In seconds, it vanishes into the woods. I wonder what frightened it.

Again, woodpecker silence. More minutes go by before the loud chatter of a red squirrel fills the air, immediately followed by a long descending bird call I do not recognize. Silence.

As I left the office for this walk a little while ago, I thought about a story I heard on National Public Radio this morning about asking people where they go to find peace. A timely story. Among the responses, I recall hearing the words "wind," "sailing," "wilderness," "hearing birds sing," and "going into a corner of a Washington DC cemetery." Every response involved some form of being in Nature as a place to find peace.

I am no different—Nature is where I go to find peace, and sanity, and a healthy escape, and a place to think—or not think. On this day, the impending war and recent news of the passing of two people I have known brought me to this hidden spot in the Mountain Park. I am reminded of the opening lines of a favorite poem by Nancy Wood: *My help is in the mountain / Where I take myself to heal / The earthly wounds / That people give to me.*

A passing jet brings my mind back to my white fir sitting spot. It is nearly dark. I am cold. The woods are completely silent—the woodpecker must have moved on, and so must I. I will take the peace that I found in this magical spot with me into my evening, and into my sleep, and hopefully, into tomorrow.

## Winter White Means Spring Green
*April 1, 2003*

I drove away from the snow-covered landscape of Beulah on the afternoon of March 21 with backpacks, sleeping bags and other gear loaded in the trunk. Destination: the desert. The precipitation had begun falling as rain on the afternoon of the 17th, switching to snow the next morning. Later in the day on the 19th, snowfall measurements in Beulah ranged from 35 to 60 inches, depending on who was reporting and what part of the valley they were reporting from. I measured 35 inches just outside MPEC. The television news reported 49 inches fell in Beulah, and I heard that someone just up the road from the park measured 60 inches. Any way you look at it, it was a good amount of snow. When I left Beulah that day, it certainly was a winter wonderland!

After several delightful days exploring the redrock canyons of southeast Utah and then soaking in the hot waters of New Mexico's Ojo Caliente, I turned off the car in my much-changed

Beulah driveway. What a difference a week makes! No, the snow was not entirely gone, but most of it was—particularly in the more southerly exposed areas. Even with another nine or so additional inches that fell while I was away, the seven-foot-plus piles of snow (I did a lot of shoveling during that storm) were gone, or reduced to barely noticeable mounds of dirty white.

And now, a few warm days later, I look around at land most certainly under the influence of spring—pleasantly helped along by many inches of moisture that just soaked into the newly thawed soil. In this small, sun-bathed clearing surrounded by tall pines where I am sitting, the winter scene of a week ago now flaunts the color green. Blades of grass, some three or four inches long, are the dominant feature of this bumpy little meadow. Polka dots of white are not snow, but the delicate blossoms of spring beauties. Of course, forty feet away in a shaded area lies a foot or more of crusty snow. Ah, springtime in the Mountain Park.

Ever since last summer's drought, I have kept a detailed record of how much moisture has fallen on this wonderful park. And I am happy to say, this winter has not been all that bad. In fact, Beulah's total snowfall this season is already a bit above average, and April, statistically our second-snowiest month, is just getting started.

The dryness of last summer was followed by 5.29 inches of rain in September and October—quite wet for those months. Then November through January brought only 16 inches of snow, containing only 1.1 inches of moisture. Pretty dry—it appeared that we were in for a repeat of the dismal winter of 2001/2002. But February was unusually wet with 43 inches of snow containing 2.91 inches of water. And March has lived up to its rank as our snowiest month with 60 inches, about 6.5 inches of moisture (and I used the more conservative 35 inches of snow from that large storm when calculating the March total). That puts this snowfall season at 119 inches. For comparison, since the winter of 1989/1990, only four of those thirteen winters had higher amounts of snowfall than this season—so far.

Of course, there's been quite a bit of chocolaty brown along with the green, as all these recent snows have made for a rather healthy mud season. Yet, I've heard few complaints about the mud this year. I suppose the drought of 2002 drove home the inseparable relationship between white, brown and green. Ah, springtime in Pueblo Mountain Park.

## Do I Get Bored Hiking the Same Trails?
*June 4, 2003*

The sun just rose over the same ridge I have watched the moon rise over many times. Its light accentuates a thin mist hanging in the creases that add texture to the treed landscape. The scene hints of the Smoky Mountains, yet I sit where I've sat a hundred times before in this park, looking at the same piece of land: Pueblo Mountain Park in the foreground, the hogback ridge and Signal Mountain behind and a small piece of the plains in the distance.

Do I get bored, spending so much time hiking the same trails? I've been asked this question many times. True enough, I've taken what seems like a million steps on the same favorite stretch of the Tower Trail that I hiked once again this early morning. But, although it is the same trail, in the same park, that is where the sameness ends. Every hike is different—sort of like variations on a theme.

The misty guise this morning is only one of the many looks that this broad scene has offered. I recall the hogback balancing a just-risen full moon, its orange color accompanied by the hoot of a great-horned owl. And the time I snowshoed up this same trail, everything covered by a white blanket of freshly fallen snow. And the time the fog was so thick there was no scenery at all. And iced trees, and the orange and red oaks of fall, and the first meandering snowflakes of the winter season gently filling the air.

Bring the scale in a little closer, say within a thirty-foot diameter circle, and the nearby landscape theme varies as well. Right around me on this late spring morning I see yellow stonecrop with swollen yellow buds, the golden blooms of senecio, a yucca's large red buds, the delicate purple flowers of a harebell (first ones this year), and several bluish-purple penstemons. Just a few weeks ago, none of this color was here. There were plenty of pink and white spring beauties though. A few weeks before that, three feet of snow covered the ground. A year ago, brown was the prominent color, as a drought was in full swing.

Oaks that were naked a few weeks ago now boast many deeply lobed leaves that are a somewhat brighter green than the nearby Douglas firs. Just the color green—there are so many variations—yucca leaves, mountain mahogany leaves, grasses, different conifers. The same? Hardly!

Then there is the auditory experience of this same place. This morning's loud symphony is dominated by the songs of American robins, western tanagers, yellow-rumped warblers, black-headed grosbeaks, with the raspy call of a western-wood-pee-wee thrown in. Add in the percussive song of a spotted towhee and an occasional squeak of a woodpecker. Except for the woodpecker, robin and towhee, all of these singing birds are migrants that arrived over the last few weeks. In January, the woodpecker squeak may have been the dominant sound, with a *chick-a-dee-dee-d*ee now and then, accompanied by the quiet *peep* of a Townsend's solitaire.

Yes, it is the same old trail, the same old park, and the same old place. On the occasion that I do find myself bored with this same old place, all I have to do is slow down and take notice of the details, and the boredom disappears. Now, an hour after I first sat down to write, I look up and notice that the mist has also disappeared—and adding to the bird symphony is the unmistakable sound of a turkey, gobbling in the distance. The same? Hardly!

## Earth Music
*October 6, 2003*

> *"The earth has music for those who listen."*
> *~ William Shakespeare*

I call this hilltop Sound Map Hill. Over the last few years, several thousand students have quietly sat here, mapping the sounds they hear around them. "Find a place to sit, get comfortable, be quiet, and listen. Make a map of the non-human sounds you hear around you." I've given these instructions hundreds of times, and most of the time, the students absolutely love to experience the peace and tranquility of simply being quiet in Nature.

And so, here I have come, to sit, get comfortable, be quiet, and listen. This comes easy for me. Of all the ways to experience the natural world, it is probably with my ears that I enjoy Nature the most.

I listen. I hear the squeak of a woodpecker flying from my right, landing on a tree branch behind me. A large fly buzzes overhead. I hear a Steller's jay from down in the ponderosas, squawking at something. A gentle breeze moves through the treetops, making a sound like a distant river. That same woodpecker just flew by, fifteen feet over my head: a quick series of wing beats, silence, a squeak with another series of wing beats, silence, wing beats, squeak. And it is gone.

A Townsend's solitaire has broken out in song down in the drainage in front of me. Another woodpecker squeaking, a chickadee's distinctive *chick-a-dee-dee-dee*, several nearby flies (one insisting that my nose is its best friend), the busy chatter of pygmy nuthatches, the ongoing drone of a cricket, yellow oak leaves rustling in the breeze, loud clicks from a flying grasshopper, a startled deer moving through the forest.

Shakespeare was right, the Earth certainly has music, if a person just slows and quiets down enough to listen. Of course, this is music. The original music, from which all music has evolved. There is melody: the lovely song of the solitaire, the chaotic calls of the nuthatches. There is harmony: the never-ending drone of crickets and the wind in the treetops harmonizing above and below all the other sounds.

And there is rhythm. In fact, Nature is full of so many different kinds of rhythm. The drumming of a woodpecker: fast and loud. The beating of my heart when I stopped for some water after hiking up a steep hill: fast and quiet. Solitaire peeps: slower, more subtle. Inhaling, exhaling: slow or fast, quiet or not so quiet. Wind rustling oak leaves: irregular, gently percussive. Night following day following night: slower still, changing incrementally. The seasons: still slower, relentless. And migratory birds coming and going; spring beauties appearing mid-winter; does with fawns gracing the woods in late spring; summer thunderstorms; trees growing old, dying, falling, decomposing, returning in new green growth; babies becoming children becoming parents becoming grandparents. Life, death, life. Rhythm.

Sound Map Hill. A place to hear the music of the Earth— which naturally leads to reflection, deep thinking, and deeper feeling. All you have to do is sit, get comfortable, be quiet, and listen.

## Thinking Like a Grandfather
*December 2, 2003*

Oct 17, 1934—the date carved into a small patch of cement on Lookout Point. A significant date to those who love to hike the trails of the Mountain Park, sit on these rocks and watch the shadows creep along the canyon walls. These rusted railings have been here sixty-nine years, one month and fifteen days. Pretty old, according to an eleven-year-old student whose class I brought here recently.

But not really. The fractured granite that these railings are cemented into formed from magma about 200 million years ago. Now that's old. Except when compared to a piece of schist I collected nearby—1.8 billion years old. Now THAT is old!

Another significant date for this park is January 15, 1920— the date these 600+ acres that became the park were purchased. I am glad there were forward-thinking people around back then with the vision to create this park. Thanks to those folks, so many people get to enjoy this park—hiking, watching wildlife, learning about the natural world.

This pre-occupation with age and the like stems from two things. The first is the geology lesson I recently developed and taught for the Earth Studies program this fall. We looked at granite and sandstone and schist (which, incidentally, I pronounced very carefully), and we walked the 4.6 billion years of the Earth's existence along a timeline. With one end of a 100-foot rope being the present and the other end representing the Earth's formation, it makes the formation of this canyon rock seem pretty recent—only 4 feet 4 inches ago. The extinction of the dinosaurs, 65 million years ago, was only 1 foot 5 inches ago. And our primitive human ancestors showed up a mere half inch ago. Now that puts things into perspective when it comes to the concept of "old!"

The second thing has to do with a more recent date that now has much significance to me—November 1, 2003, the date my daughter Sierra gave birth to Jude—and the date I became Grandfather Ranger Dave.

Among the many things this event has me reflecting on as I sit on this rock, watching the day grow older, is what this park—and this world—will be like as Jude grows up and lives his life. If he were to retrace his grandfather's footsteps to Lookout Point on January 17, 2073—sixty-nine years, one month and 15 days from today, what will this mountain landscape look like? And this trail—will it still be a narrow hiking trail? What about the landscape between Beulah and Pueblo—will there still be ranches, and pronghorn, or will it be nothing but houses?

Such thinking makes me wonder if we, today, are making the kinds of forward-thinking decisions that will allow Jude to grow up and live in a community, a country, a world where he can hike and readily see landscapes like the one right here—tree-covered hills of ponderosa and fir forests, with not one house or road in sight. Decisions that may have him stepping over a frozen bear scat full of acorns as he hikes this trial in 2073. Or he'll examine a large 4-toed track in the snow and think, "Maybe a mountain lion came through here last night. No, it shows claws, and it's not round like a cat's. Maybe it's a wolf. It could be," he'll wonder, because he'll know that wolves were successfully restored to Colorado when he was still a young person. He'll smile, knowing that the land is intact—and healthy. And he'll silently thank us for making such wise decisions.

A brisk wind brings me back to the present. As I hike back down the trail, I will send a silent thought of thanks into the wind for the wise decisions made years ago, that will allow me, in a year or so, to take Jude on his first hike with his grandpa in this wonderful Mountain Park. And maybe he'll get to see some bear scat too!

## Searching for Spring
*January 31, 2004*

One minute I am trudging through snow above my ankles, the next I am traveling on a snowless dry trail. It's the snow-free areas underneath the oaks that are the focus of this morning's hike. Or, more precisely, a delicate, five-petaled, pinkish-white flower that first appears right around now. *Claytonia rosea*— spring beauty. Last year's first blooms were discovered on January 27, the earliest in the last six years. I usually find the first blooms sometime during the first two weeks of February.

Such careful observation reveals many other things going on out here on this gray winter day. Beneath dried asters are clumps of tiny new leaves that together look like a bumpy green pin cushion. Many of the mountain mahogany branches, with buds primed and ready to become this year's crop of green growth, still sport several feathery spirals, each attached to a seed. A most lovely tree ornament, even if the tree is a scraggly winter shrub. Another pleasing sight is the sickle-shaped seed heads of blue grama grass atop a yellow-dry stem poking through the crusty snow.

I could go on and on—tracks, bird calls, scat—such a rich diversity of life, or biodiversity, in this foothills park. In fact, I recently learned that the nearby Squirrel Creek Canyon has the highest diversity of tree species of any one place in Colorado.

A sad reality of our times creeps into my thoughts anytime I think about biodiversity. On a global scale, it is disappearing. So many species have become or, are on the threshold, of becoming extinct. The rate of extinctions is, according to most researchers, at least one thousand times the normal rate of extinctions.

Species extinctions are nothing new, some might argue. Species have always disappeared; even high rates of extinctions are a part of the history of life on Earth. True enough. But what makes the current mass extinction different is that this time it's not being caused by an asteroid hitting the Earth, or extreme volcanic activity. It is being caused by the activities of one species—*Homo sapiens*.

I am reminded of watching a television news journalist introducing a story several years ago on a building project that was being held up by the project's potential negative impact on an endangered species of mouse. It was obvious, and unfortunate, that the journalist thought this was a ridiculously silly situation—not allowing a huge building project because of some little rodent. My thought then, and now, is simply, where do we draw the line? If people are, indeed, making life and death decisions for entire species (and not just individuals of a species), by what criteria do we decide what goes and what stays?

Aldo Leopold said it well over fifty years ago:

> The outstanding scientific discovery of the twentieth
> century is … the complexity of the land organism. Only

those who know the most about it can appreciate how little is known about it. The last word in ignorance is the man who says of an animal or plant: "What good is it?" If the land mechanism as a whole is good, then every part is good, whether we understand it or not. If the biota, in the course of aeons, has built something we like but do not understand, then who but a fool would discard seemingly useless parts? To keep every cog and wheel is the first precaution of intelligent tinkering.

Back to what I came out here to find: are spring beauties blooming yet? Apparently not. My careful inspection of the oak duff does reveal many of its fleshy leaves, dark green, magically turning the sun's energy into new plant tissue, even in January. But no flowers, or buds. I'll keep watching for this harbinger of the spring that is still many weeks away. It's a tough job, but somebody's got to do it.

## Small Is Beautiful
*April 1, 2004*

My view from this "couch" made of reddish granite takes in most of the Beulah Valley and a wide V-shaped chunk of the plains. I can see Highway 78 and the landscape it traverses, nearly all of Pueblo, and a large expanse of open country north and east of Pueblo. A hundred square miles or more compose the macro-view from this rocky perch.

I then turn and focus on a couple square inches of the granite that supports me. My careful look reveals more colors than just red—several shades of red, pink, black, and gray, with tiny quartz mirrors reflecting the sky's light. A light green lichen is made up of individual lobes with a peach-colored center that reminds me of a mushroom from the cover of the Allman Brothers' album *Eat a Peach* (*You're my blue sky / you're my sunny day...*). Scurrying on erratic paths are orange creatures smaller than the head of a pin. Probably some sort of mite. Watching their movements closely, I notice a second scurrying creature, this one brown, longer, but thinner than the other. Another mite?

All too often, so many of us are as oblivious to this endless micro-world right under our noses as these mites are to the hundred square miles viewable from this piece of granite. For many, appreciation of Nature is usually towards the macro. Yet so much of the beauty and wonder of Nature is found in the countless micro-worlds that surround us, everywhere and anywhere. This seems more so for adults—young children are more apt to notice the small tadpoles in a puddle or the insects under a log. But the tendency is to miss the magic of the little details as we grow older and move faster, for individuals as well as for society.

Being aware of the micro is one of the joys of having learned to slow down. And the world of flowers, especially small wildflowers, provides so much beauty and wonder in such compact packages. Back on the trail, I discover that a little member of the mustard family, the mountain bladderpod (*Lesquerella montana*), came into bloom the last couple of days. The bladderpod is one of the year's earliest wildflowers to bloom, and these late winter/early spring wildflowers are always a thrill to find, announcing that I'm nearing the end of another winter. Not that I dislike winter, but truth be told, I am always ready for spring when it arrives.

So here I am, lying face down on the rocky trail, focused on one of the plant's four-petaled flowers, a half-inch wide, yellow as the skin of a perfectly ripe unbruised banana. Aided by a 10x magnifier, I spy a tiny, skinny insect that is as black as a moonless night—but many times bigger than the granite mite I saw earlier—just hanging out among six stamens with dull yellow anthers swollen with pollen.

Further along the trail, I discover that another mustard, mountain candytuft (*Noccaea montana*), also came into bloom the last few days. Its quarter-inch blossoms of white petals house six stamens with anthers that look like tiny striped cucumber beetles.

The newly emerging leaves of the hairy golden aster (*Heterotheca villosa*), which will not bloom until midsummer, provide another micro-sight worth stopping for. Every leaf is covered by countless silvery hairs, softer than the softest down. Each flower, each plant, each insect, each leaf—whole worlds of incredible delight, ready to be discovered by anyone willing to slow down and take a look.

E.F. Schumacher was certainly right, *small is beautiful*. I know, I know—his classic book was about economics, specifically, "economics as if people mattered." But the "small" in Nature is beautiful too.

## Merging Landscape with Mindscape
*June 8, 2004*

A hot day has driven me to the shady north-facing hillside that overlooks the Devil's Canyon Trail. This is an ecosystem of tall dense Douglas firs and white firs, a cool refuge from a relentless sun. The forest floor is exceptionally green thanks to prolific April snows. Sun-dappled grasses, ferns, tree seedlings, and a few flowering plants—sugarbowl, fleabane, chickweed, false Solomon's seal—a giant multi-textured quilt embracing me on this midday saunter.

I am not alone on this cool hillside. From the trees a pair of western tanagers sound as if they are talking to each other. "I'm here, where are you?" "I'm over here, where are you?" Back and forth they converse. And there is a flycatcher (not sure of the species), a red-breasted nuthatch, and an Audubon's warbler. A small spider takes a short walk across my leg before returning to the blade of grass from which it came. A tiger swallowtail butterfly teases me with occasional glimpses as it flits about in search of nectar like a drunk in fast motion. No doubt there also are larger animals nearby—deer, maybe a bear—comforted as I am by this shady hillside.

This land has become a part of me—I have inhaled molecules of oxygen that have literally come out of these trees and other plants. And I have become a part of this land—carbon from my exhalations is used by these green plants to grow, to become more of themselves. This land and I share more than just the physical. I am reminded of a line by author and essayist Barry Lopez, "The interior landscape responds to the character and subtlety of an exterior landscape; the shape of the individual mind is affected by land as it is by genes." Lopez speaks eloquently of how the quality of a person's thoughts is, as author David Orr put it, a "merger of landscape and mindscape."

This is why so many people turn to the outdoors to recreate and, by default or by design, to think. We walk, we jog, we hike, we fish, we hunt, we saunter—and we often do some of our best thinking outside. It is why I always try to do much of my writing outdoors, as my thinking and, hence, my words, are as influenced by where I am as by anything else.

And this is why there is a Mountain Park Environmental Center. As an educator and Nature education center director, I cannot do anything about the genes of the children who attend our programs, but it is the "exterior landscape" of children's educational experiences that I can do something about.

I hear the voices—and now the footsteps—of a group of MPEC campers hiking down the Devil's Canyon Trail, completing the Northridge Trail loop. It pleases me that the diverse ecosystems of Pueblo Mountain Park through which they just hiked are becoming a part of these young people's interior landscapes. For many, I know, it is their first exposure to what could be called "wild Nature." I can hear in their voices that this experience is fun for them, as summer camp should be. It is also vitally important to them, as an exterior landscape of only man made landscapes is not only sad, but dangerous. Dangerous to them because lives devoid of experiences in the natural world are lives devoid of the multitude of physical, mental and emotional benefits Nature can provide. And dangerous to the land, because a people brought up without experiencing Nature first-hand are much less likely to grow up and advocate for the land. We protect what we love, and we love what we know.

Veteran teacher Diane Stewart recently wrote about the experience of her students in our Earth Studies program for fifth graders:

> I have heard my students say that they will never just walk through a forest again without thinking of the life that is under their feet and surrounding them in the trees. They have a respect for nature now and know that it is up to them to preserve what they have. The learning that has taken place will not just be for this year but for a lifetime.

Yes, this is why there is the Mountain Park Environmental Center.

*Dave Van Manen*

## Wilderness With a Capital "W"
*July 23, 2004*

Its horizontal flanks of gray-looking alpine tundra, possibly with some lingering patches of snow, are hidden by the low clouds of a midsummer upslope. Greenhorn Mountain, named after a Comanche Chief slain at its base, still stands tall at the southern end of the Wet Mountains. I just can't see it! If I were atop its 12,347-foot summit right now, chances are I'd be in the sunshine, above an endless blanket of low-lying clouds. I'd also be in the middle of an officially designated Wilderness Area, one of more than 600 units set aside by the federal government where "the earth and its community of life are untrammeled by man."

The first paragraph of what is known as the Wilderness Act reads:

> In order to assure that an increasing population, accompanied by expanding settlement and growing mechanization, does not occupy and modify all areas

43

within the United States…leaving no lands designated for preservation and protection in their natural condition, it is hereby declared to be the policy of the Congress to secure for the American people of present and future generations the benefits of an enduring resource of wilderness."

Wilderness advocates across the country are celebrating the Act's fortieth anniversary this September, as it was signed into law on September 3, 1964, by President Lyndon Johnson.

Wilderness means many things to many people, but Wilderness (with a capital W) has a specific meaning within the context of the law. As the opening sentence states, lands that are designated as part of the National Wilderness Preservation System are meant to be protected in their "natural condition" so there exist places that are a refuge from the unnatural conditions of cities and other developed areas. As such, certain activities are not allowed in Wilderness areas: commercial enterprises; roads; use of motorized vehicles, motorized equipment or motorboats; landing of aircraft; mechanical transport; or structures. What is allowed is foot and horse travel, fishing, hunting, and all other non-mechanized forms of experiencing the natural world.

Needless to say, there were—and still are—opponents to the concept of Wilderness. To set aside land in its primitive condition, to "lock it up," not allowing logging or other extractive activities, to prevent the use of motorbikes or ATVs, is wrong, according to these folks. But the numbers speak to these criticisms: only 2.5% of federally owned public land (all Forest Service, Bureau of Land Management, Fish & Wildlife and National Parks land, excluding Alaska) is designated Wilderness. The other 97.5% of federal land does not have these protections. (If you include Alaska, 4.6% of federal land is Wilderness.) Not all that much land is "locked up."

It could be argued that it is a wise and forward-thinking people that decides to protect some of its country's land in its natural state. It could even be argued—and is argued—that 2.5%, or 4.6%, is not nearly enough land protected as Wilderness. The benefits of Wilderness are many: reservoirs of biological diversity; scientific value; watersheds; critical habitat for wildlife and plant life; historical and cultural value; spiritual value; aesthetic value; and a refuge from our fast-paced industrial society. And, economic value. Accurate and honest analysis indicates that wild lands left undeveloped often have higher and more sustainable economic value than lands exploited for commodities.

The state of Colorado and, indirectly, Pueblo Mountain Park, have strong links to the history of Wilderness preservation. It was Arthur Carhart, a Forest Service planner who envisioned the creation of Pueblo Mountain Park, who strongly recommended in 1919 that the Trappers Lake area in northwest Colorado be preserved in its natural state. In his words:

> These areas can never be restored to the original condition after man has invaded them, and the great value…should be available, not for a small group, but for the greatest population. Time will come when these scenic spots, where nature has been allowed to remain unmarred, will be some of the most highly prized scenic features of the country.

The Forest Service decided to follow his recommendation, and Trappers Lake remains wild to this day, part of the Flat Tops Wilderness Area.

Every time I look at Greenhorn Mountain, I feel a glimmer of hope. Greenhorn represents the fact that we, as a society, *are* willing to place some limits on our activities. The very concept of Wilderness—land that is "self-willed," where Nature, not man, is in charge—indicates self-restraint on the part of people. And this gives me hope that maybe, someday, we will ultimately decide to heed the words attributed to Chief Seattle, that "the earth does not belong to man; man belongs to the earth."

**Ecology and Economy—Two Views of the Same Thing**
*July 26, 2004*

When you think of the field of ecology, what comes to mind? Trees, soil, birds, climate, forests, insects, flowers…earthy kinds of things, right? You probably do not think of concepts like throughput, production and consumption of commodities, externalities, and other terms of economic theory. Well, the times they are a-changin'—at least, they ought to be. Ecology and economics are essentially just two different ways of looking at the same thing.

Ecology is the study of how the "Earth household" works; or, more precisely, the study of the relationships that connect all members of the Earth household. Economy has to do with the management of Earth's material resources, especially as they relate to satisfying people's needs and wants.

In essence, economics has as much to do with trees, soil, and insects as does ecology. After all, it is the Earth that provides all the raw materials that move through our economic system—and absorbs its wastes. Unfortunately, neoclassical economic theory does not include the natural world in its formulas and calculations. Most economists do not factor ecosystems, soils or other basics of the planet's ecology into their calculations and projections—as if the human economy functions completely independent of Nature.

Our economic system was designed at a time when the planet seemed infinitely large, and human economic activities were comparably quite small. In that large empty world, the vision of the "macroeconomy" (all small "microeconomies" added together) functioning in a seemingly limitless world appeared to work. It was simply a given that the world was big enough to provide all the raw materials that moved through the economy and be the "sink" for its wastes.

Here at the beginning of the 21st century, this given is no longer, well, a given. The biophysical reality is that the Earth has limits. Like it or not, the macroeconomy is not an isolated flow of abstract exchange values that can grow forever and ever. Human economic activity is really just a subsystem of the finite natural world.

For any economic formula to be truly accurate, it must factor in Nature. As former World Bank economist Herman Daly put it, "The macroeconomy is an open subsystem of the ecosystem and is totally dependent upon it, both as a source for inputs…and as a sink for outputs." It may not have seemed so in the mid-1800s, but we should have learned by now that natural stocks like forests, soils, water and wildlife are finite, as is the ability for the Earth's systems to absorb our wastes. If the formulas of our macroeconomy do not factor in the Earth's natural capital and absorptive limits as it grows and grows and grows, it is, as Lewis Thomas called it, "stupidity on the grandest scale."

Many believe that human ingenuity, manifest most clearly in

technology, will enable us to overcome any constraints that are, according to Julian Simon, "merely biophysical." In fact, economist Robert Solow believes we can "get along without natural resources." (But would we want to?) It is true that our technologies enable some degree, sometimes significant, of stretching, and even overcoming (or so it seems) physical limits. But, as our species' impacts on the Earth's natural systems continue to grow, we are seeing that this is true to a degree, but *only* to a degree. Basic ecology teaches that all ecosystems have a carrying capacity, and when that carrying capacity is reached and surpassed, the system will attempt to self-correct, one way or another. As it is often said, Nature bats last.

The obvious question for economists is, "How big should the subsystem—the economy—be relative to the overall parent system, the Earth?" Any honest search for the answer certainly must involve those who know about the planet's ecosystems— namely, the biologists and ecologists and others well versed in the Earth's natural systems. And if the answer means that our economy should have quantitative limits, then isn't it time we heeded that and redesigned our economic systems to fit the world—instead of trying to get the world to fit the economy?

Think of it this way: The next time you are walking onto an airliner, imagine how take-off will be if the plane is loaded beyond its carrying capacity. Will you feel safe flying on a plane run by a company that decides to ignore the plane's limits?

The Earth is an airliner, too, and it has its limits.

## I am Most Alive in the Treetops
*September 30, 2004*

I've been telling myself I would get up here just to sit and look and write for weeks now. Finally, here I am. At 7400 feet above the level of the sea, the hilltop on which this recently refurbished Fire Tower sits is the Mountain Park's highest point. And the view does not disappoint from this windy perch. The patches of aspen on the high ridge to the southwest, in colors ranging from light green to bright gold, with small amounts of orange and red, stand out against the backdrop green of ten thousand conifers.

The opposite direction's vista expands from the park in the foreground, to the Beulah valley, then out onto the plains to Pueblo and beyond. The blue waters of Pueblo Reservoir, as well as the dam, are visible, much clearer with binoculars. I watch the shadows of the sky's small cumulus clouds slowly move across the landscape, lazily drifting across the flats, sliding in and out of the land's folds and creases. Pikes Peak sits to the right of a saddle to the north. A red, sparsely treed mountain creates the left rise of the saddle, its shape looking like a dormant volcano. I can almost see steam spewing from its cone top, so volcanic does it look to my eyes.

Along with a 360-degree panorama, the top of the Fire Tower offers a treetop glimpse of the nearby trees that I do not get with my feet on the ground. At eye-level with the top of a 40-foot ponderosa, I am watching the upper branches dance in a rather strong wind. Shining needles are playing with the sunlight in a way I've never noticed from below.

Suddenly the wind just stops, as if someone pulled the plug on a giant fan. I can practically taste the quiet. Now I can hear the *peep* of a Townsend's solitaire, the nasal *yank* of a red-breasted nuthatch, the alarm of a red squirrel, and the wing beats of a passing Steller's jay. For some reason, the jay appears much bluer than usual.

It flies by a Douglas fir tree heavily laden with cones. A close look at the tree reveals that the branches growing towards the north and east extend nearly twice as far from the trunk as those growing in the opposite directions. I look around and the same holds true for most of the trees. The return of the wind reveals why. The trees on this hilltop have lived their 50- 60- 70-plus years—and grown their branches—with frequent-enough winds to have pushed these branches in the direction the wind usually blows. The wind usually comes from the southwest, just like it is today. These winds have stunted the branches that try to grow into them, favoring growth in the direction the wind blows toward.

Such are my discoveries during this time in the treetops. The wind's return, along with the shadow of a larger cumulus cloud, encourage me to return to the ground. But I will be back. Terry Tempest Williams says we are most alive when discovering. If that is so—and I think it is—then this time spent 35 feet off the ground, with panoramic views, playful needles, dancing branches, drifting cloud shadows, a bluer than blue jay, powerful winds, palpable quiet, forest sounds, and some careful observations, has been time full of life for me. I look forward to my next opportunity to sit atop this Fire Tower and watch, listen, think, and discover. And be richly alive!

## Patriotism as if the Land Mattered
*October 9, 2004*

"What this park needs is some patriotism." With these words, the park caretaker raised a new U.S. flag on the recently painted and repositioned flagpole on that late fall day in 2001. Like many Americans, he was feeling the need to express his love and devotion for his homeland in those difficult and confusing months following September 11.

What he did not recognize, I suppose, is that with or without the flag, this park—its very existence—is all about patriotism. That our predecessors would set aside these 600-plus acres of our homeland, where the natural world could go about its business, build and maintain trails and other simple infrastructure where citizens can enjoy Nature, recreate, and find refuge from the ever-increasing frenzy of our culture, is absolutely an expression of patriotism. And the work that he does, taking care of this little piece of our homeland, is also patriotism, in action.

After all, our country is just as much the very land it occupies as it is the government, laws, cities, and citizens. The dictionary definition of *patriotism* is "a feeling of love and devotion to one's own homeland." Accordingly, acts of love and devotion to our nation's forests, prairies, seashores, rivers, mountains—and its parks, from Yellowstone to Pueblo Mountain Park to a small acre of urban greenery—are patriotic acts.

There is much talk these days about "homeland security" and defending our nation from threats, particularly terrorist attacks against citizens and key infrastructure. One law purported to that end is called the "Patriot Act," so strong is the connection between patriotism and protection from threats. Since our nation is made up of many facets, including its diverse landscapes, then actions that threaten the ecological health of these landscapes are also threats to our homeland security—in a sense, another brand of terrorism. For it is the very land that has molded and continues to mold the character of this nation, and it is the land that sustains, inspires and nurtures its citizens. Damage the land and you damage the nation. Hence, the efforts of countless conservationists—paid and volunteer alike—who seek to protect the ecological integrity of our homeland are also, by definition, acts of patriotism.

It is a sad sign of our times that much of our media-driven culture, including the political processes presented by most media, seems to overlook the fact that conservation is a fundamental expression of patriotism. Clearly, flying flags and saying pledges are portrayed as patriotic acts. That protecting and conserving the home*land* itself is somehow not on the patriotism radar-screen demonstrates just how far removed our culture is from this most fundamental expression of love and devotion to our country.

Such lack of recognition of the patriotism inherent in conservationist efforts is also a significant reason, maybe the main reason, why a growing consensus of scientists believe that our planet—and, hence, our nation—is in an ecological crisis of proportions unprecedented in the history of our species. One manifestation of this is our nation's unwillingness to seriously address the many potentially catastrophic global environmental issues of our day (e.g. global climate change, destruction of biological diversity). As retired Air Force Pilot Reese Liggert recently said, "I was in the military because I think it is very important to defend the country. I'm in the Sierra Club to make sure there is something worth defending." This all seems to logically mean that to act in a way that damages or diminishes the natural environment is actually unpatriotic.

The time has come for us to bring conservation and protection of the natural world into the mainstream definition of patriotism. As Alaskan Richard Nelson clearly put it, we need

> a patriotism based on ecological knowledge, moral consideration, ethical principle, spiritual belief, and a profound love of the earth underfoot. I believe this is the most basic, most urgent, and most vital patriotism of all, because conservationists are working in service to the elemental roots of their existence, as human organisms, as members of their communities, and as citizens of their nation's land.

## Loving Winter, Still
*November 29, 2004*

*Cold, and it's getting colder / Gray and white, winter all around / And oh, I must be getting older / All this snow is tryin' to get me down.* These lyrics from an early John Denver song have been floating around my chilly brain while I hike through this powdery new snow. When I began this hike, the storm that dropped about a foot of snow on the park was still managing to produce some snowflakes. It was, as the song says, *gray and white, winter all around.*

Now, two hours into the hike, the gray snow clouds have pretty much given way to a sky of a few clouds with some blue to add to the afternoon color scheme. What little sunshine that made it through was weak at best. It has now slipped below the western ridge. *Cold, and it's getting colder* is now the most appropriate lyric.

The blanket of clouds that turned the park into a world of whipped-cream-covered everything also provided some insulating effect, holding in a bit of modest heat. With the clouds dissipating, the thermometer that barely managed to make it into the mid-teens is now on its way down. I can feel the cold working its way through my layers of fleece and wool as I write these lines, like water droplets of a summer storm working their way through layers of branches until they finally reach the still-dry forest floor. Yes, it is going to be a cold night!

I've been watching the seasons change for nearly a half a century, and I still find it nothing less than fascinating. My journal entry for November 18 reveals that I found a blooming mountain candytuft (*Noccaea montana*) along the Devil's Canyon Trail. A small cluster of four-petaled flowers, creamy white against a backdrop of rich green, spoon-shaped leaves. It was still warm and light and gentle enough for this plant to produce flowers. Eleven days later, a dozen inches of cold snow. It is now, unarguably, winter.

John Denver may have spoken accurately of the winter landscape, but his lyric of *all this snow is trying to get me down* does not speak for me. I may be getting older, but I still love winter. And I have every expectation that I will continue to love winter as I get older. No, I don't like driving on snowy, icy roads. But the winter landscape offers so much to discover, and notice, and marvel at. And I've discovered the key to enjoying winter— getting out in it!

The story being told by the tracks in the snow indicates that I am the only human "getting out in it" along the Tower Trail today. But I am not alone. Several deer have been zigzagging through the scrub, looking for something nutritious in this winter landscape. The nibbled twigs of a mountain mahogany shrub indicate that they did find something worth eating.

Another set of tracks does not reveal much detail due to the soft snow, but the size and shape of the track pattern has me thinking fox or bobcat. I follow until I find some detail in some shallower snow beneath a ponderosa pine. The presence of nails says canine, as feline tracks seldom register nails. The size has me believing a red fox—not the smaller gray fox—has been through here not too long ago.

I can feel my facial skin tingle as the temperature continues to drop. I try to balance my close-up observations with some brisk walking to keep the warm blood flowing. Each step produces a squishy sound as my boot crunches the snow. But it is hard to keep moving as there are so many little works of art that demand my attention. Dark leafless branches of Gambel oak supporting large wads of cottony snow. Drifting flakes from a falling snow clump, backlit by golden clouds illuminated by the already set sun. The paths of snowballs released from low branches and rolling various distances down the gentle slope above the trail. A vertical slab of orange granite checkered with a chaotic pattern of yellow, green and gray lichens, framed by white powdery snow.

Yes, it is winter once again—and I love it still!

## Finding Comfort in the Changing Seasons
*February 1, 2005*

> *"In a way winter is the real spring, the time when the inner*
> *things happen, the resurge of nature."*
> *~ Edna O'Brien*

The electricity is down. The phone doesn't work. The road is impassable. Such is the plight of many of us two-leggeds after the skies dumped thirty inches of heavy wet snow on Beulah over the last few days. (I measured 30 inches, although I've heard reports of nearly double that). A better excuse to get out I couldn't have. So, I strapped on a pair of snowshoes and set out to inspect the nether reaches of the park.

The storm was hard on the park's ponderosa pine trees. Unlike the flexible branches of the firs, the large bulky branches of the ponderosas are obviously not as well adapted for bearing heavy loads of snow. Scattered in the deep snow were large broken branches, their long needles adding some green to the white groundscape. Not only branches, but here and there were nearly entire trees snapped off along their trunks, leaving broken-topped snags that will eventually become avian condominiums, thanks to the park's resident woodpeckers.

I trudged up the trail to a familiar fallen snag that should be getting good sun this time of day. A little snow removal (I've done plenty of that the last few days), and here I am, warm and comfy at my afternoon writing spot. I am right next to the place where, on January 19, I discovered the year's first blooming wildflowers (eight days before the earliest I've recorded them in bloom). It has become an annual pilgrimage of sorts for me, to seek out, in the middle of winter, signs of the spring that is still several weeks off. In a way, seeing those delicate pink and white spring beauties in bloom, a few short weeks after the winter solstice, says to me that right here, in this little spot beneath a few scrawny oaks still clinging to a few brown leaves, it already is spring.

It occurs to me that what I am seeking when I search for January wildflowers may not really be spring at all. There is great comfort in witnessing for myself that this winter will be followed by spring. Maybe what I am seeking is not spring specifically, but that feeling of well-being that comes from knowing that the ancient cycling of the seasons is continuing. There may be many other things I cannot count on during these uncertain times, but the turning of the seasons I can count on.

In essence, what season is approaching is not really the point. I find no less comfort in seeing winter's first snowflakes drifting out of a gray autumn sky. Or the first sound of thunder from an approaching storm on a warm afternoon in late May. Even this storm, its heavy snow typical of a late March storm, hints that this winter holds the approaching spring in its grasp.

I look up from my page and see that, despite those nearby flowery signs of spring, the land still says winter quite loudly.

But I know that, thirty feet away from my sitting spot, buried beneath many inches of snow, spring is already geared up and ready to burst forth. Yes, the cycling of the seasons will continue for another year.

## Thinking about Pinyon Pines, Drought, and Yellow Flowers
*March 28, 2005*

I call this cluster of rocks along the Mace and Tower Trails loop Lower Tranquility Rock, as opposed to Higher Tranquility Rock (or Couch Rock, as some folks refer to it) along the Northridge Trail. I've been coming here for years, to sit, think, plan, contemplate, dream, and sometimes, just to be. When faced with a difficult decision about some serious challenge when raising my children, I would come here, looking for, and often finding, clarity. When formulating plans to create the Mountain Park Environmental Center, this rock was my "thinking place." When troubled by some disturbing or sad news, I would frequently find solace here.

And so, once again, here I sit. In spite of some big things going on in my life, I am pleased that, right now, on this warm breezy day, nothing in particular is on my mind. I seem to have a kind of free association going on—I look at something, like a patch of mud, and I am sent off in some direction of thought sparked by the mud. Then I notice an interesting looking cloud, and off I go in another direction.

I look up from the page and see a pinyon pine. It looks green and healthy, unlike the countless pinyons along the road to Ojo Caliente Hot Springs. A recent drive through southern Colorado and northern New Mexico for a quick getaway to Ojo's hot waters revealed mile after mile of mostly dead pinyons, weakened by the drought and killed by the ips beetle. I look around and count nine healthy pinyons, a little island of healthy trees, right here surrounding Lower Tranquility Rock.

I hear what sounds like a red-tailed hawk. But something tells me it is a Steller's jay, performing one of its many mimics. Yup, there is the trickster's handsome blue in the green of a nearby ponderosa pine. I've been fooled before, but not this time.

The snow that was covering the trail has melted into a tiny river that is sliding its way down a section of the orange-pink granite that was once liquid itself, a long, long time ago. The ten inches of snow that fell a couple of days ago is rapidly going the way of the other 117 inches of snow that has fallen on the park this winter. This is the third consecutive winter of above-average snowfall in the park (only slightly above, so far).

I am reminded of some of the reading I've been doing lately. One thing I've learned is that, despite these rather wet years, most of the western United States is still in the grip of a drought. According to dendroclimatologists (scientists who look for climate patterns in the growth rings of trees) and other paleoclimatologists (those who study ancient climate using glacial ice, lake- and sea-bottom sediments, corals and tree rings), droughts have been a common occurrence during the last 1,000 years of western U.S. weather. Not only the occasional dry year, but 20-plus-year droughts, lengthy stretches of very sparse precipitation, sometimes with a few wet years in between. The science indicates that widespread forest fires accompany these dry stretches. The science is also saying loud and clear that these patterns are being exacerbated by the irrefutable fact that the planet is getting warmer, due largely to greenhouse gas emissions from human activities.

I think back on a river trip I took down the Colorado River into Lake Powell two summers ago, and how the lake level was 40 feet below the "bathtub ring" of a full reservoir. Lake Powell is now 33% full. Scientists have realized that the 1920s, when Colorado River water was divided up among seven western states, was an unusually wet decade in the river's watershed. Many are beginning to believe that Lake Powell may never be full again. The common occurrence of droughts, rapidly growing Southwestern cities, and a warming planet all point to some very challenging times ahead.

Such are my thoughts on this early spring day. For me, it is important to be informed about such issues, but I need to be careful because I can easily wind up in a hole of despair about the sad realities of our time. I have found that I must balance my awareness of such issues with the hope and joy that comes from experiencing wild Nature. I think of the advice of Edward Abbey, "Save the other half of yourselves and your lives for pleasure and adventure. It is not enough to fight for the land; it is even more important to enjoy it." So, I look up and find myself back in the moment. I see an almost-blooming mountain bladderpod and remember that, just an hour ago, I discovered the year's first bladderpod in bloom. Its many yellow flowers, small but radiant, were the color of the sun come to life in the petals of a little mustard. "It's going to be a great spring," I think to myself.

## The Happy Return of an American Dipper
*June 1, 2005*

It was a warm enough afternoon one day this past March, so I decided to sit on the rock wall above the park's mostly frozen main pond and jot down a few thoughts in my journal and, mostly, just enjoy being out. I looked up every now and then to see what was happening around me. It was on one of these looks that I spotted a slate-gray bird standing on the edge of the ice next to the open water at the pond's inlet, doing what appears to be quick little deep-knee bends. These *dips* are one of the ways to identify the American dipper, a robin-sized bird that simply loves the water.

Also known as a water ouzel, *Cinclus mexicanus* reportedly only hangs around mountain streams that are pollution-free. Its absence in the park the past six or seven years made me wonder just how clean the park's creek really was. So, to say I was pleased to see this large wren-like bird back in the park would be an understatement. I was thrilled!

I watched as it flew over to a dried cattail, then back over to the ice. Then it dove into the ink-black water and disappeared. The American dipper has what is probably the most unusual foraging strategy of any songbird in North America. A consumer of small fish, insects, and possibly aquatic plants, a dipper will sometimes wade along the shore, often with its head underwater. But its preferred method of searching for food is to walk along the bottom, completely submerged. As the authors of *The Birder's Handbook* state, "Amazingly, these birds are able to forage on the bottom of streams in which the current is too fast and the water too deep for people to stand." It gets to the bottom by "flying" underwater, capable of reaching depths of 20 feet or more.

After half a minute or so, the bird re-appeared and flew right onto the ice again, dipping away and looking no worse for its late winter swim. In fact, these birds are designed for being in water, even in the iciest of conditions. Their dense soft plumage is very difficult to saturate, while an additional eyelid is utilized to protect the eye from dirt suspended in the water.

Since my late winter encounter with this interesting bird, I've been on the lookout for it. Is it here for the summer? Does it have a mate? Or was this just a lucky sighting as it was passing through? On an after-dinner walk yesterday, under a pastel sky that had just cleared after three days of on again/off again rain, I heard a loud melodious birdsong coming from the spillway below the park's smaller pond, just a couple of hundred feet north of MPEC. Sounding as happy as any creature could sound, that wild melodious song answered a couple of my questions loud and clear—at least one American dipper has taken up residence in Pueblo Mountain Park. Further snooping revealed a second bird, so it looks as though we have a breeding pair of dippers in the park. Somewhere along the stream that has been brimming with snowmelt for several weeks, maybe along the shore in some rocks, maybe even on a midstream rock, there should be a mossy nest, hopefully holding several white inch-long eggs.

Long before my first sighting of an American dipper many years ago, as it flew just above the raging waters of an early summer creek in the Sangre de Cristos, I learned of this bird through a wonderful essay, *The Water Ouzel*, by John Muir. Muir was also quite fond of the "mountain streams' own darling, the humming-bird of blooming waters." What I remember most from this delightful essay brimming with affection for this amazing bird is his description of its singing.

> Among all the mountain birds, none has cheered me so much in my lonely wanderings,—none so unfailingly. For both in winter and summer he sings, sweetly, cheerily, independent alike of sunshine and of love, requiring no other inspiration than the stream on which he dwells. While water sings, so must he, in heat or cold, calm or storm, ever attuning his voice in sure accord; low in the drought of summer and the drought of winter, but never silent.

Welcome back, hummingbirds of blooming water. The park has missed you, and so have I.

## A New Story Begins
*August 3, 2005*

Several weeks of hot dry weather. Decades of fire
suppression in a fire-dependent forest. A long-term drought.
Unnaturally dense brush. A lightning strike from a dry
thunderstorm. Very low humidity and erratic winds. Any one of
these could be a story by itself. But, as John Muir plainly put it,
everything is connected. So, when all these smaller stories got
connected the second week of July, a very big story began to
unfold. I am now heading up to the place where this connection
happened, known as the Mason Gulch Fire burn site.

The fiery connection ignited a flurry of human emotions—
fascination, fear, anger, terror, gratitude—plus the countless
human stories that will be told for decades. And, hopefully, it
offered some long-needed education about living in fire-
dependent forests. But my goal today is not to consider another
human story. I am here to read for myself the first few lines of a
brand-new story—the story of this land in the aftermath of one

of Nature's most incredible forces—wildfire.

I hike the half-mile to this transformed landscape through dense thickets of Gambel oak, then open grassy areas, underneath a canopy of mostly ponderosa pines. Everything is green. There is no visual evidence of the fire, so I am following a compass reading determined by referring to a map of the burn area. Before long, the air offers assurance that I am getting closer, as I pick up the strong, unmistakable scent of things that have burned. *Many* things that have burned, as revealed when I approach the burn site.

Once inside the perimeter of the burn area, black becomes the dominant color. After wandering around a forest of scorched tree skeletons for a while, I am now sitting atop a flat rock large enough to keep me from the charcoal remains of things that were alive and growing just a handful of days ago. And I gaze in awe at the transformation that recently took place here.

Although the landscape is dominated by the black remains of ponderosas and oaks, it becomes obvious that the fire did not burn uniformly across the mountainous terrain. There are islands of brown-needled pines. The heat was apparently hot enough to cook the green out of them, but not hot enough to torch them like many of the surrounding black snags. Some trees even show green amidst the brown needles, although surrounded by a sea of lifeless remains. In some places, oak branches still cling to brown, fire-tinged leaves, and the pines are only superficially burned a few feet up their trunks, their branches still alive and well. Such is the nature of wildfire, burning with abandon here, only fingering along the ground there. Looked at broadly, the 11,357-acre burn site is a mosaic of varying burn severity, some areas burned hardly at all, some moderately, others scorched right down to the mineral soil.

The raucous call of a Clark's nutcracker changes my focus.

I add this large jay to the list of birds I've already seen or heard here: western wood peewee, Steller's jay, northern flicker, hairy woodpecker, broad-tailed hummingbird. The rocks, so much more noticeable and prolific without the green understory to hide them, grab my attention. Mostly white sandstone, some as large as cars, show varying shades of black from the flames that licked their sides. The many cracks, fallen flakes, and broken pieces illustrate that fire should be on the list of forces that break down rocks!

I've seen many species of ants and spiders busily being alive on this lifeless land that really isn't so lifeless. Deer tracks punctuate the blackened soil. The story is unfolding.

The rock where I sit has an eight-inch-tall spreading dogbane plant growing next to it, complete with green leaves and, amazingly, flowers. A small white butterfly flutters from one bloom to another. In some areas, dozens of dogbane plants are sprouting from roots that survived the fiery storm. Oak leaves, some already 6 inches long, sprout from the barren ground. Even in the places where the fire burned down to bare soil, there are grasses, dogbane, and several other species beginning the process of healing this altered landscape.

Yes, the land says it clearly—wildfires are destructive. Read a little deeper, though, and it also says fires are natural. In fact, fire has been a factor in shaping nearly every plant community in every bioregion in America. However, this fire, burning in a low-elevation forest type that hasn't been allowed to burn in way too long, was so much more destructive than it should have been.

The Mason Gulch Fire lasted little more than a week, but the effects of it will be evident on this land for decades, even centuries. Had fires been allowed to burn every five to ten years or so in this forest, like they did for thousands of years prior to European settlement, the disturbance would likely have been much lighter. Even so, the land will recover—evidently, the recovery has already begun. The story being told here today on this burn site, less than three weeks after containment, is again captured by the words of Mr. Muir: "By forces seemingly antagonistic and destructive Nature accomplishes her beneficent designs—now a flood of fire, now a flood of ice, now a flood of water; and again in the fullness of time an outburst of organic life."

## A Forewarning
*October 4, 2005*

A gust of wind momentarily drowns out the drone-like call of a Townsend's solitaire. I am not sure what the bird is saying, but this wind has a message. It is a forewarning of a cold front that right now is sitting on the Colorado-Wyoming border. Each gust speaks of a change that is about to occur.

My hike today is in early fall—it is warm, even hot and, and in spite of the wind, there is a gentleness to match the sun-dappled hillsides donning bright autumn shades. But the wind says that this won't last. Tomorrow's hike reportedly will feel like late autumn. Never mind what the calendar says—it is the thermometer and the rain gauge that determine what season each day's walk is in. If I want to be out walking in gentle early fall, then today's the day! Early fall may return again in a few days—and maybe not.

After a morning of one office task after another, I finally could wait no longer—I had to get out and hike. At first, although my body was walking in the sunshine, my mind was still back in the office. But then, a gust of wind, a whiff of an earthy aroma, the sight of burgundy autumn chokecherry leaves, and I left the office behind—in mind as well as body.

Hiking up the hill to the trailhead had my heart pumping. My eyes were soaking in the brilliant fall colors that I know are such short-lived delights. In no time they'll be gone. As my feet left the road and took the first few steps on the trail, I noticed a profound change. The gravelly crunch was immediately replaced by soundless steps on the soft, needled tread of the trail. It was like sliding from the surface of a lake into the underwater world below. By leaving the road, I entered into a deeper layer of the natural world.

After thirty minutes of hiking, I am now sitting on a sunny hillside, watching the shadows of racing clouds slide across the land. Here in the shade of a pinyon pine, inhaling its sweet fragrance, I am so glad I pried myself from my desk. Admittedly, it was not easy to do—I have lots more work waiting for me back there. What helped is this realization that has been popping into my head more and more lately—the fact is, I am not going to live forever.

With the big "Five O" just around the corner, I often find myself contemplating the fact that, statistically, I have more days behind me than I have left ahead of me. My hunch is that this is not a unique realization—most people probably have similar thoughts as life's statistical halfway point slips by. What's important, at least for me, is what comes from this awareness. Too many people, it seems, live as if they're going to live to be 150, or 200. They put off, they procrastinate, they wait until later. And then, they wake up one day and it's late. Maybe even too late.

Just like these winds telling me a change in the weather is

on the way, this recurring realization is another forewarning, a reminder of sorts, telling me that the ultimate change is also on the way for this mortal body of mine. Hopefully, not very soon, but change, no doubt, is coming. So, if walking these trails on a gentle autumn day, and on rainy days, and cold snowy days, is important to me—and it is in many more ways than I can say— then I'd better keep prying myself out of that office. I think I'll just sit here a while longer, inhaling the sweet pinyon, these autumn colors, this glorious day.

## Where The Road Ends
*November 30, 2005*

A few moments of calm allow me to realize how warm the sun is. But here comes another blast of cold wind, which the warmth of the sun is no match for on this chilly late fall day. I'm tucked under a scrawny juniper that is heavily laden with berry-like cones on a rocky south-facing hillside just outside the park's western border.

Being off the ridge, the wind is just tolerable enough and the sun is just strong enough for me to sit and enjoy the solitude that this remote spot offers. From where I sit, I can see no buildings, no roads, no fences, not even the trail—no sign of civilization at all. Yet, less than an hour ago, I was sitting in my office with its computer, phone and other gadgets that keep me ever so connected to the human-centered world that I, and most of the rest of us, spend the bulk of our time in.

I've always considered this 611-acre park as a place where civilization and Nature meet. Not that civilization is without

Nature—in fact, human communities are 100% dependent on the natural world. But the park still represents a meeting place of sorts between the human-dominated and non-human-dominated worlds. At the park entrance, the paved highway becomes a dirt road. Move through the eastern part of the park, past a few buildings and stone bridges, and soon the road ends. Continuing west, the human imprint on the land is limited to a few narrow foot trails. Leave the trail behind, as I have right now, and civilization seems very far away.

In fact, this pinyon / juniper hillside comprises a small part of what is called the Scraggy Peaks Roadless Area and begins at the park's western boundary. Devoid of roads and automobiles, Pueblo Mountain Park's backyard roadless area is 27 square miles—about 17,500 acres—of mountainous terrain dominated by wildness. It is an accessible yet wild place where people can find respite from the human-made world. It is a place where people come to hike, bird, hunt, fish, backpack, and enjoy the solitude that is becoming increasingly difficult to find as each year slips by. It is also part of the watershed that provides water for many creatures, including people.

I applaud the fact that this land, being National Forest, does not belong to any one individual or family, but is owned by all Americans. Yet, when I am out here, I get this feeling that this land is not really owned by people at all. This land belongs to the wild community of plants and animals that live out their lives on this rugged land. People are sometimes a part of this wild community, but essentially only as visitors. Like this juniper tree I am tucked under—it is providing me a bit of temporary shelter this afternoon, but several scats that I found nearby, composed entirely of juniper seeds, illustrate that this tree provides life-sustaining nutrition to the creatures that live here. I'm the visitor—it's their home. Even if I do spend lots of time and feel quite at home here, I'm still just a visitor.

That this land remains roadless does, indeed, deserve applause. In a civilization that often seems to believe that people and their vehicles should be able to go anywhere they want, this wild land illustrates a restraint that is in too short supply in the human relationship to Nature. It answers yes to environmental activist Dave Foreman's far-reaching question, "Do we have the generosity of spirit and the greatness of heart to share the earth with other species?" What makes a human community "civilized" is the recognition that some limits are necessary for the collective well-being of the community as a whole. Our relationship with the wild natural community also requires limits if we are interested in living sustainably and well into the 21st century and beyond. Sure, we *can* build roads in here, we *can* continue to build an economy that requires infinite growth on a finite planet—but, we do so at great cost to the natural world, and ultimately, to ourselves. Look at one of the costs, clearly illustrated by Hurricane Katrina, of choosing to destroy the wetlands along the Gulf coast over the past several decades. Kept intact, wetlands provide coastal lands with protection from some of the destructive impacts from hurricanes.

The relentless wind is winning over the weakening sun. It is time to end my afternoon visit to this wild place. I happily return to the human-centered world, because I know that this wild landscape is here for me and my fellow humans to visit, and for so many other species to live their wild lives in. My hope is that this Scraggy Peaks Roadless Area remains wild and roadless so in fifty years, my granddaughter, who was born a few weeks ago, will be able to hike up through the park and experience the same solitude as I have found here today.

## Such A Good Question
*January 31, 2006*

"Don't they have a right to live, too?" This question, asked by a fifth-grade girl earlier today, is with me as I trudge my way through the mud and sloppy snow of the Mace Trail. After a day of teaching mammalian biology, an introduction to cardio-vascular exercise, and ecological concepts such as carrying capacity and predator-prey relationships, it feels good to be out by myself. Even with the sun nearly gone, this mid-winter day is still mild and gentle.

Earlier, in a sunny classroom bordered by a stand of Douglas firs, the students were discussing wolves, including the subject of reintroduction. I was pleased that an otherwise unruly bunch of students were fully engaged in this discussion that was sparked by another question, "Should wolves be reintroduced to the wild places of Colorado?"

After talking about Little Red Riding Hood, the successful restoration of wolves to Yellowstone National Park and the subsequent ecological benefits, whether I could carry three of these students on my back up to the Fire Tower (as a way of introducing carrying capacity—we surmised that I couldn't), the migrating 2-year-old Yellowstone wolf that made it as far as I-70 in the summer of 2004 (where it was killed by traffic), and ranchers' concerns about wolves killing livestock, the words of this student seemed to strike a chord in her classmates.

"Such a good question," was my response.

Later in the afternoon, as I enjoy my late-afternoon hike, I find myself thinking deeper into her question, which I have asked myself countless times before. Truth be told, we all ought to be asking ourselves this question. Why? Because how we, as a society, answer the question, "Don't they have a right to live, too?" will, in my view, speak loudly to the kind of world our children and grandchildren will live their lives in.

The worldview that has dominated the human-Nature relationship for the last several centuries seems to answer the question with, "If they are useful to humanity, only then do they have a right to live." Or, as Gifford Pinchot, first director of the U.S. Forest Service put it 100 years ago, there's only "resources and people." A century of this worldview, supported by ever-more-powerful technologies, has, according to so many scientists and thinkers, brought many of the world's natural systems (upon which all human and non-human life are wholly dependent) to the brink of unraveling.

My vision for the future is that we soon learn to answer this question in another way, guided by "the silent cry of wilderness, of wolf, whale, forest and ocean alike, 'See me for what I am, not as you wish to use me.'" These words by author Michael W. Fox represent an ecocentric, or biocentric worldview that, as Aldo Leopold so clearly articulated, "changes the role of *Homo sapiens* from conqueror of the land-community to plain member and citizen of it."

79

My hope is that we abandon the human-centered view—that the world was created solely for humans, and the planet is managed to accommodate human wants and needs only. It is past due that we, as a species, recognize that we are one among a large network of interconnected species. "A network," according to environmental scientist Donella Meadows, "is nonhierarchical. It is a web of connections among equals." When our perceptions, values and choices reflect these realities of the natural world that we are an inseparable part of, only then will we answer that fifth-grader's question with an answer that allows for the well-being and flourishing of both human *and* nonhuman life.

## Living In Awe
*March 2006*

"Looks like you'll have the whole place to yourself. This is the only backcountry permit we've issued. Have fun!" With these words from the park ranger fresh on my mind, I strap on my pack and begin a four-day solo in the 23,000-acre wilderness of northern New Mexico's Bandelier National Monument. A few raindrops and 30 minutes of easy walking and I have left the developed part of the park behind me, including the ruins that are the park's main attractions. Not that I am disinterested in these incredible remains of a centuries-old thriving Indigenous village, but I am here for other reasons.

I am hiking up Frijoles Canyon, hopping back and forth across the partially frozen creek every few minutes. Frijoles Creek, which will be my water source for the next several days, has been eroding prolific deposits of "tuff"—rock comprised of ash from nearby volcanic activity—for thousands of years. As the ash solidified, countless air pockets created natural cavities in the soft rock, the larger ones becoming the cliff dwellings of the native peoples that called this area home up until about 450 years ago.

The trees are all very familiar to me, dominated by ponderosa pine, Douglas fir and white fir. Replace the tuff with pinkish granite, and I'd think I'm hiking the Devil's Canyon Trail in Pueblo Mountain Park. Ground-dwelling plants that include holly grape and grama grass, accompanied by plenty of Gambel oak, make me feel right at home.

After five miles of hiking, with camp set up and water bottles filled, I have the afternoon to do whatever I please. With a warmth-eating shadow already beginning to envelop my campsite, I scramble up the east side of the canyon and find a large flat rock on which to enjoy the remaining sunshine. A canyon wren sings its lovely melody as I notice some feelings of loneliness that often accompany the early hours of a solo. "More and more I am realizing the natural world is my connection to myself," says Terry Tempest Williams. Loneliness is a good sign—without the distractions of the peopled world I left a little while ago, I am much more aware of the natural world I am immersed in, and I am much more aware of myself. That's why I have come to this wilderness.

Satisfied after a simple dinner, I am sitting just outside my tent, dressed warmly for a chilly evening, writing with gloved hands. The air is perfectly still. The ponderosa pines surrounding my campsite are black silhouettes against a still-bright but quickly fading western sky. I am facing an exquisite waxing crescent moon, the illumined sliver gently cradling, like a cupped hand, the remaining pale orb, faintly lit by Earthshine. A few small white clouds lazily drift by.

The loneliness has already morphed into an overriding sense of pleasure, basking in the solitude and beauty of this place. In a few days, I will turn 50. I am here in this wilderness to turn 50 deliberately. Just to have reached this age seems impossible —I was just 30 the other day, hiking the Tower Trail with my two young kids. A few days before that, I was 15, contemplating life on a lonely beach on eastern Long Island. How could I be 50?

\* \* \*

These wilderness days have come and gone, and now my backcountry solo is nearly history. In an hour or so, I will hike out of here and return to the people I love, my work, my life. I have hiked, explored, watched birds. I have done a lot of thinking. "To live life fully, to avoid devoting your whole life to accomplishing things, you have to be aware of death." "Everything is transient. Without that awareness, how can you truly live in awe of what you see—the seasons, the sun." Not that I expect to die any time soon, but, with 50 already here, these words by Lorry Nelson ring wise to me.

Accomplishing things. Living in awe. I think I am pretty good at accomplishing things. One thing I've landed upon during these wilderness days is that, as much as I may continue to get things done, I do not want "accomplishing things" to be the dominant theme of my life in my post-50 years. It is the idea of living my life always in awe—of white volcanic cliffs full of ancient air pockets, of the mystery of Indigenous peoples hidden in the ruins of their village, of the crescent moon graced by lazy clouds, of the song of the canyon wren, of the eyes of my grandchildren as they watch birds at the feeder, of three decades being married to my teenage girlfriend—this is what I am drawn to.

So, I take with me from this wilderness experience a renewed realization that it is my love for the people in my life and my love for Nature that are responsible for so much of the meaning in my life. These loves make me the person I am at the half-century point in my life. I take with me the intention that "living in awe" will be the dominant theme of my life after 50. Thank you, Bandelier National Monument, for a most meaningful 50th birthday!

## Reflecting on the Drought
*June 2, 2006*

What I consider the park's best singer is filling the woods with the happiest of bird songs. I know, science says that the song has nothing to do with being happy; it is simply a male black-headed grosbeak defending its territory, keeping other males from its mate. But my ear has a difficult time equating such a glorious melody with anything but a creature that sounds delighted to be alive, sharing its joy with all the world.

The air is also filled with the sweet-scented vanilla of ponderosa pines warmed by a sun that is now hidden behind some welcome afternoon clouds. I glance up at a graying cumulus cloud and find myself hoping for rain. Like most everyone else around here these days, the thought of drought is never far from my mind.

In the past couple of weeks, I have heard people say, "If it doesn't rain soon, the creek will be dry in a week!" "It's going to be the worst wildfire season yet!" "It's as dry or drier as it was in 2002!" So many of the conversations I have, and hear, include concerns such as these. It seems as if so many of us are living with ever-present worry about the drought, like a heavy coat that we can't seem to take off. Including me!

Lately I am growing weary of it, and I am seeking to rid myself of this burdening coat of heaviness about the drought. A little research has me chewing on these facts: 93% of the time, at least five percent of Colorado experiences a three-, six-, twelve-, or twenty four-month drought; three-month droughts occur approximately 90 of every 100 years in any given location in Colorado; long multi-year droughts have occurred in Colorado's past as a natural part of long-term weather patterns; since recording weather statistics began in the late 1800s, the years 1982 through 1999 had above-average precipitation and were the longest drought-free period; the 1990s were the wettest in southeastern Colorado history.

A lot to chew on. If my response to drought is going to be dominated by a heaviness that is always ready to take a hold on me, then I may as well get used to it. Because the reality is, I live in a semi-arid part of the world where drought is as much a part of the landscape as vanilla-scented ponderosas and the melodious songs of black-headed grosbeaks. The wetness of the two decades leading up to the present drought was an anomaly in a land that is normally much drier. And, despite the many downsides to drought, allowing it to get me down is still a choice, a choice that I make.

Knowing the truth about drought helps me recognize another choice: accept the fact that I live in a place where drought is a normal part of the landscape. Yes, the dryness may be exacerbated by global warming (increased drought length and persistence is consistent with the latest global warming projections). Yes, wildfires are more intense due to global warming (increased drought creates drier fuels) and mistaken forest management (fire suppression which has only increased fuel loads in forests). But this is still where I live, and being down about it is a drag.

I look up to see that graying cloud no longer appears to hold much of a possibility for producing rain. But the grosbeak is still singing away. Maybe there's a message in that bird's happy song. After all, right now he lives in the same place that I live, yet his song sounds as if he hasn't a worry in the world. I think I'll just sit here and listen for a while.

## It is Time to Let Go of the Myth
*July 27, 2006*

Kinnikinnik full of bright red berries. Hairy golden aster everywhere. Goldenrod. Nodding onions, some 18" tall. Hairy four o'clock just beginning to bloom. One Kansas gayflower with its spike of feathery light purple flowers. The season's first smooth aster. Dark red chokecherries. Sunspots and ragleaf bahia, two common summer daisies, just beginning to add more yellow to the land. Patches of blue grama grass boasting a healthy yield of seeds that grow sideways off the top of the stem, looking like a crop of thin mustaches, brown at the top, bleached blond below. Three-feet-tall Pacific sagewort.

This is just a short list of the plants that caught my eye on this morning walk. All in response to the prolific rains of the last several weeks, which are a result of early monsoon moisture. And an arrangement of low- and high-pressure systems, and a jet stream, favorable to bringing moisture to these mountains. All influenced by water temperatures in the Pacific Ocean along the equator, many thousands of miles from these flourishing plants.

In contrast, the old, weathered rock that I am sitting on appears unfazed by all the rain. True, the process of turning this rock into mineral soil may have been furthered slightly, but I can't see it. The lizard that lives around this orange granite probably benefits from the increased insect population brought about by the rains. The two healthy deer buck I saw earlier are positively impacted by the moisture, as all the grasses provide excellent forage. And the young doe I had a staring contest with the other day (she ran, I won) will grow stronger with so much good food. Next year, she may produce two healthy fawns, and both may survive into adulthood.

And to think, all because of the ocean temperature a world away from this park. No doubt, these temperatures are influenced by a multitude of factors, some within the understanding of our science, some outside of it. To say it is complex is an understatement. To say we understand how it all works is simply not true. To say we're going to manage it—well, that's a joke!

Yet, we try to manage the Earth's forests, and oceans, and air—all components of the global weather system that we understand rudimentarily at best—as if they belong to us, and us alone. Our actions manifest the dominant cultural assumption that humans are the superior species, the rest of the planet is here for us to use at our discretion, and it is our job to manage the Earth. Our culture teaches a dualism with humans on one side, everything else on the other. It says that, in essence, we are separate from the rest of Nature. We are the planet managers.

I don't buy it. So much of what I see and hear, and my intuition, and this 200-million-year-old granite—all tell me this is wrong, and dangerous, thinking. Looked at historically, it is actually new thinking. For most of human history, our species lived with a much humbler view of our place in the world. I believe the future well-being of the Earth requires a profound shift in our species' view of our place in the world towards a whole lot more humility, and an acceptance that we are only one among many species. In the 1994 words of author and professor T.H. Watkins:

> If we allow ourselves to put aside our arrogance long enough, perhaps we can read the lesson written in the eyes of lizards and deer deep in the land of stone time: this world and its creatures were not presented to us; we were joined to them in the exquisite saraband of life. The arrangement was never meant to be a conquest, and it is more deeply complex than a responsibility. It is a sharing.

The voices, both human and nonhuman, telling us that we need to move beyond this dualistic view of the world are getting louder. Just listen to the news. Something is very wrong. The dominant culture's worldview is analogous to a young child who hasn't yet learned to share. It's not all just for him/her. It is time—past time—for the human species to let go of the myth that we are the superior species in charge of the rest of the planet. This does not mean that we are not an incredible species, capable of incredible things. We are. We're clever—just look at our inventions. We're capable of intelligence, and reason, and beauty, and compassion. Just listen to Mozart, or read Emerson, or think about Mother Teresa. And we're capable of sharing, with each other, and with our nonhuman neighbors. But it is time we seriously redirect our incredible capabilities into managing what absolutely needs managing. Ourselves.

## Listening for the Stories
*October 5, 2006*

I spent last weekend at a gathering of grassroots activists who work for the land—protecting it, studying it, teaching about it, writing about it. We were camped in Professor Valley, a wide red-dirt valley about twenty miles north of Moab in southeastern Utah's quintessential canyon country. Much of the spirited conversation was about the power of the written word in inspiring and assisting our work for the land. What Gatorade is for the runner, inspired writing is for the activist.

The redrock canyons of southeastern Utah have a healthy list of eloquent writers who have written volumes about that desert land. Several of them were among us at this memorable event. I am one of many who have learned to love those canyonlands of our western neighbor state. The words of these writers have played no small part in nurturing my relationship with that land— and all land.

Today, a few days after leaving that redrock country, I finally have some time to be out on the land that has been the focus of so much of my work. Yes, I so enjoy spending time in those redrock canyons, but my heart remains in this square-mile piece of southeastern Colorado known as Pueblo Mountain Park, a place where the built and natural landscapes meet. I have spent much of my time since I've been home thinking, writing, talking and lobbying for a part of the "built landscape" of this park—the Horseshoe Lodge. As I write these words, my back, still tired from too many hours of driving this past weekend, is finding comfort as it leans against an adobe wall of this historic building.

The Horseshoe Lodge is a great old building—a great old building that just sits here, doing pretty much nothing but accumulating cobwebs. Occasionally, a group uses it for a day or two, but then its 14,000 square feet are empty again, day after week after month.

Some say that if you sit near the Lodge for a while, sit very quietly, like I'm doing right now, you just might hear the stories it has to tell. It has lots of stories. Like how it was built back in the 1930's by CCC and WPA crews happy to be working on a great project. Like how it was part of the vision of a young man named Arthur Carhart. Carhart believed that the American people should get out and enjoy our country's National Forests and learn about the natural world. The Beulah area, with its easy access to the San Isabel National Forest, was the very first place in the country to give his idea a go. And the Lodge would provide a base from which people could get out into our public forests. You might hear stories about how the Lodge used to have hundreds and hundreds of people, especially children, using it just as Carhart envisioned.

And if you listen even closer, you might hear how the Horseshoe Lodge is not happy sitting here by itself. It misses all those little feet scampering across its floors. Some folks say they've even heard the Lodge itself whisper that it is thrilled about MPEC's plan of moving into the Horseshoe Lodge— "It's about time," it says.

Our plan is pretty simple. MPEC's popular programs have outgrown our current building, so we're going to move into the Horseshoe Lodge. But the Lodge needs some serious work before we can move in. The renovation will be a "green" phased project that will create multi-purpose rooms, a spacious interpretive center, upgraded overnight facilities, and a major overhaul of the downstairs kitchen and dining areas. The ultimate result will be a simple yet tasteful, four-season overnight facility. It will help MPEC fulfill the vision of Arthur Carhart by allowing for a whole new menu of programs, including retreats, trainings and longer, more comprehensive environmental education programs.

As a lover of landscapes and a lover of language, I have at times been tempted to uproot and join the ranks of the articulate dwellers of Utah's redrock country. I can't deny it—it is a seductive landscape. But such thoughts always lead me back to the realization that this land of ponderosa pines, pygmy nuthatches, and an historic old lodge is the land that I belong to. This is the land that is my home. This is the land that I am supposed to protect, study, teach and write about.

For a while longer, I'll just sit back against these old walls, look out on these tall pines, and quietly listen for the stories this old building—and these old trees—have to tell. I have a feeling I'm going to be sharing these stories for a long time. And that suits me just fine.

## A Quiet Intimacy with Nature
*December 1, 2006*

I've been reading about Charles Darwin when he was a young naturalist:

> He watched and recorded, for every bird he saw, its manner of walking, perching, flapping, and resting. All of this was rooted in the naturalist's stillness that Darwin had begun to cultivate.... But Darwin was developing a lighter touch ... Darwin made himself small, and quiet, and patient.... Darwin spoke with a simple warmth toward his subject; he had entered into a quiet intimacy that allowed him ease and facility beyond the cool objectivity of pure science. Here, in patience, in stillness, the birds show themselves and tell their secrets. The stories are not shaken out of them beneath a microscope but revealed, animal by animal, with a kind of earthen familiarity, on the forest soil.

These insights into Darwin's development as a naturalist are from a wonderful book by Lyanda Lynn Haupt, *Pilgrim on the Great Bird Continent.*

With these images of the young Darwin fresh in my mind, I set off for an early afternoon on the trail. I've been cooped up in the office for way too long, doing way too much, so here I am. Quiet intimacy. Naturalist's stillness. Earthen familiarity. The language used to capture Darwin's unfolding as a naturalist is familiar and comforting to me. For all that being in Nature can be, it is the still, quiet intimacy that I seek more than anything else.

So, here I am again, sitting on this same rock where I've sat hundreds of times, with the same hogback ridge providing the same backdrop to the same trees in the foreground—a rocky mountain juniper, a scraggly ponderosa behind it, a pinyon pine. This week's foot of snow does add a nice touch of white to it all—a touch I've seen many times on this land.

Being perfectly still, a species of bird I've watched numerous times lands within a few feet of me. I can plainly see the white eye ring of a Townsend's solitaire before it flies off to the juniper, then to a leafless oak, then up to the top-most branch of the ponderosa. A pine squirrel chatters from below—a sound I know well. I have an "earthen familiarity" with this land. Yes, I keep coming out onto this same land, but, like Darwin's birds, the secrets of this land are revealed very slowly, over many years. It is the patient naturalist that learns them, so I keep returning, in patience, in stillness.

Learns a few of them, anyway. For, in truth, this land contains infinite ways of revealing itself. Barry Lopez writes in *Arctic Dreams:*

Whatever evaluation we finally make of a stretch of land, no matter how profound or accurate, we will find it inadequate. The land retains an identity of its own, still deeper and more subtle than we can know. Our obligation toward it becomes simple: to approach with an uncalculating mind, with an attitude of regard. To try and sense the range and variety of its expression—its weather and colors and animals. To intend from the beginning to preserve some of the mystery within it as a kind of wisdom to be experienced, not questioned. And to be alert for its openings, for that moment when something sacred reveals itself within the mundane and you know the land knows you are there.

A lone raven circles nearby. I watch its large, rounded tail pitch from side to side as it maneuvers a graceful turn in a strong breeze. The breeze hits me and I immediately notice my cold and stiff fingers. Time to move along. I think I'll head down the Mace Trail—for only the thousandth time or so. As I hike, I notice a large ponderosa snag just east of the trail. Halfway up is a perfectly round hole, the work of a woodpecker. The snag has been there several years—I recall looking at it many times. But I've never seen the hole before. Odds are, it was there the last several times I hiked here, but only today is this subtle feature of the land revealed to me. I make a mental note to add this to my list of nest cavities that I'll observe next spring. And if I'm small, and quiet, and patient, I just may get see a pair of bluebirds, or nuthatches, busily tending a new brood. And I'll enjoy a quiet intimacy with this expression of the land revealing itself to me, and I'll know that the land knows that I am here.

## I Love to Climb Trees
*April 3, 2007*

I heard a short National Public Radio report this morning about how young people are not climbing trees these days. It also mentioned the rise in repetitive-stress injuries among young people, the result of countless hours manipulating the controls of electronic games, fingers making the same small movements again and again and again.

So, I set out on a hike on this breezy spring day thinking about the many downsides of kids spending way too much time plugged in, but mainly, thinking about climbing trees. I love to climb trees. At least, I did when I was a kid. I recall a particular tree in the woods behind my family's summer place on Long Island that was "my tree." I spent countless hours in that tree. There were several branches near the top that created the perfect perch for my small body. I can see it now, a 10-year-old me, in my tree (and a whole lot of other trees), doing just what a 10-year-old ought to be doing up in a tree—using my whole body to climb it; learning about and challenging limits, both mine and the tree's; seeing rabbits and dinosaurs and bears in the drifting clouds; daydreaming; thinking about life in my secret treetop spot. As I jog my memory, I think I would even read up in that tree.

Little did I realize then, but all those hours in that tree would have a significant impact on how I live my life—what I do for recreation, what I do for a living, and what I am doing right now at this very moment. No, I am not up in a tree (although that sure sounds like a good idea). But one of the lessons I learned perched in that treetop—that spending time alone in Nature is a healthy way to sort through thoughts and feelings—is why I set out on this hike today.

Recent awarenesses in my own life, and recent unfoldings in the lives of some of the people in my life, have me dealing with a hodgepodge of ideas, thoughts and feelings that keep bouncing around inside of me. Some of it hurts, some of it seems nothing but unfair, and some of it keeps coming back at me, demanding I do something about it. So, after a vigorous walk, here I am, sitting in the sunshine, surrounded by a cluster of trees serving as an effective windbreak on this warm and windy day. As I've been doing since my childhood in the treetops, I have come out here to think, to feel, to plan, and to try to make sense of some things in this world that just don't make any sense. And, along with all this mental activity, I am here to enjoy being a part of this land, and to release, at least for a little while, the shackles of an overactive mind and experience the peace that Nature can bring.

I've been coming out here long enough to know that, although I may not, today, or ever, find all the answers I seek, or gain an understanding of some of the senselessness that comes with living in this world, coming out here is still a very good way to seek answers and find a bit of comfort. And, along the way, the emerging song of spring, with its wildflowers beginning to add color to the land, its birdsong filling the air, its wind dancing with the trees, and its blue-sky sunshine filling my eyes, makes me glad that I got to climb trees when I was a boy.

Being out here also has me wondering if all those kids playing video games, planted in front of a monitor screen for countless hours, will, as their future unfolds, find the same source of solace from their electronic games as I find out here among the trees. I doubt it!

## The Mason Gulch Burn Plus Two Years
*June 12, 2007*

I'm out of breath as I climb the steep hill that leads to the burn site. I haven't been here since last October, with a group of students studying fire ecology. It's almost two years since I first found my way into the southern portion of the Mason Gulch Burn, guided by the burn's charred smell not too many days after the fire was officially out. Since then, the shoes of over 500 students have created enough of a trail that navigating is easy. Several deer have evidently been using the trail since the last group of students was here last fall. Oops, I've lost the trail. In spite of all those feet, there's less trail than I thought.

With most of the climbing behind me, the land has leveled near the burn. No charred smell today as I walk through a forest of ponderosas and green grasses, the last unburned stretch before entering the burn. There is a conspicuous absence of wildflowers in this unburned forest, unlike the first part of the hike, which was a bit more open. I enter an edge area that burned at a low intensity. The green of the grasses is punctuated with flowery color: the blue of low penstemon, pink wild onions, white and yellow fleabane daisies, bright orange wallflowers, and gold golden banner. There's even a red-stemmed spotted coralroot growing next to a lightly charred but still healthy ponderosa. Some of the Gambel oak that was nipped by flames has recovered, sporting many green leaves. Oaks that were hit harder by the fire have new leafy branches growing from their roots, some four feet or taller. Several conifer seedlings are poking up here and there.

A western wood peewee's scratchy song from farther into the burn encourages me to continue walking. Forest Service data indicate that 68% of the burn was severe, 31% burned moderately, and only 1% was lightly burned. I nearly step on a fox scat. A poke with a stick reveals several small rodent bones. Walking into a section that burned severely is like walking into a wild onion farm in which the farmer let the grasses get out of control. And not only onions and grasses—wallflower, penstemon, milkvetch, senecio, and skullcap are everywhere, with black tree skeletons standing like tall scarecrows. I proceed deeper into the burn and find an area with less grass, more exposed soil, and some different flowers, especially scorpion weed. Wooly mullein, considered a noxious weed and found pretty much everywhere in Colorado, is widespread. A few more steps, and dense grasses again dominate with dozens of tall western wallflowers showing off their pretty orange blooms. Ponderosa pine seedlings can be found here and there.

Every ponderosa snag shows evidence of woodpecker activity, exposing brown bark as they chipped away the black, and surprisingly thin, charred veneer. Large white mushrooms appear to be oozing out of several large snags. A few blackened trees have had their trunks broken off by strong winds 15 to 20 feet above the ground. The remains of juniper trees are losing much of their blackened bark, becoming the silver sentinels that will remain here for years, witnessing this land continuing its post-fire life.

After exploring for a couple of hours, I find the same white sandstone boulder I sat on when I first visited 23 months ago. I climb up, take an apple out of my pack, and survey what was an inferno, and then a virtual moonscape, in July 2005. Right now, it would be hard to call this a destroyed landscape. From where I sit, a riot of green has taken over this land, interrupted here and there by white sandstone boulders and the bright colors of flowering plants. Hundreds of burned snags remind me of the forest that was once here, and the forest that will once again grow here, decades from now when the conifer seedlings grow tall.

My focus has been on the ground, where, along with dozens and dozens of plant species, I noticed prolific deer sign. Looking down most of this time, I haven't seen the many birds that I've been hearing—hummingbirds, juncos, woodpeckers, house wrens, spotted towhees. So, my plan is to put the journal away, take out my binoculars, and find my way out of here spying some of the bird life that is hanging around the burn. The flames certainly changed this land, but there is no question that this land, two years after the Mason Gulch Fire, is brimming with life.

## The Stories This Tree Could Tell
*July 24, 2007*

*All the flowers of all tomorrows are in the seeds of today.* A weighty thought, this Chinese proverb, as I head for the shade of a huge ponderosa pine for a bit of respite from the hot sun on this afternoon hike up the Mace Trail. The size of the tree distracts me. Easily 150 years old. That would put its earliest years of life as pre-Civil War.

If this tree could talk, would it have stories! Like the one about a Ute hunting party that camped nearby when it was only twenty feet tall. Or the one about a young grizzly bear that rubbed its back against the tree's 40-year-old bark. Or the last wolf howls it ever heard on a cold snowy night almost a hundred years ago. If this tree could talk, it might tell of the enthusiastic voices of people who walked through these woods in 1920 as they talked about plans for a place called Pueblo Mountain Park. Or the CCC crews of young men who found work carving out the new park's foot trails in the 1930s, and the excitement in the voices of so many young people who hiked those trails in the many decades that followed. Ah, the stories this tree could tell.

Old trees like this one may someday tell the story about how these young, excited voices began to disappear from these woods when children stopped spending much time outside in Nature. A trend began in the last few decades of the twentieth century, the story would go, when young people preferred being "plugged in" to being outside. At the same time, childhood rates of obesity, depression and attention disorders began to climb, some to crisis levels. That's the beginning of the story. The end of the story hasn't been written yet.

As I started this hike, I passed a group of MPEC campers playing in the creek. Several were building a dam, two or three were looking closely at something in the water, and one was squealing for a reason I couldn't decipher. This, I thought, is how kids ought to be spending a hot summer afternoon. Which is what got me thinking about that Chinese proverb.

And this. At a meeting I attended yesterday, a veteran biologist with the Colorado Division of Wildlife (CDOW) talked of the serious lack of interest among young people in working for the CDOW. Not that long ago, he said, 1000 applications would come in for 15 new positions a year. This year, only 68 applied. Only eight of the 15 positions were filled due to most applicants being unqualified.

Lack of interest in and inadequate qualifications for natural resources employment. Lack of outdoor time among children. Other twists in the trees' unfinished story. If the current trends continue, it one day may be decided to eliminate wildlife biologists altogether. A hint of one way the story could go. But there is another way.

All the flowers of all tomorrows—that is, every future flower—are in today's seeds. So those seeds must be treated with the utmost care. If we care about all the children of all tomorrows, and if we care about the Earth, then we must treat the children, and the Earth, with the utmost care. Aldo Leopold talked of "the seed of the love of nature" that is in all people. We owe it to our children, and to the Earth, to reverse these dangerous trends and do whatever it takes to nurture "the seed of the love of nature" in ALL children—by getting them outside to experience Nature's lessons and wonders and adventures, to learn to bond with and love the natural world.

Then the trees' unfinished story could continue with the excited voices of children once again filling the woods. And those who really learn how to listen to the stories of these old trees may even hear them whisper the wisdom of Walt Whitman, "Now I see the secret of making the best person: it is to grow in the open air and to eat and sleep with the earth."

## I Go There to Disappear
*September 27, 2007*

They say that the Horseshoe Lodge project just might make me go crazy. Building plans. Electrical. Mechanical. Historical. Cost projections. Capital campaigns. Design decisions. Pile it all on an already full plate of programs, and I might slip off the deep end, they said.

With these thoughts in my head, I look out across a narrow valley of spruce and fir trees, speckled with golden aspens, and I remember: thought-stop! The warm sun on my arms, cool with sweat as I take a break on this steep ascent of the Comanche Trail, drives home the point. I am here as an antidote to the craziness that could, if I allow it, get the best of me. There will be plenty of opportunity, and need, to think about all those details. But I'll deal with them more effectively if I can walk away from them now and then. So, here I am, walking away. But, as I've learned many times before, getting the body away is the easy part. It's the mind that so easily slips back into fray. So, thought-stop!

The scenery helps. Helene dropped me at the trailhead, on the eastern edge of the Sangre de Cristo Wilderness, an hour ago. The plan is to meet her on the other side in a few days. There's about 15 miles of solo wilderness hiking between now and our meeting spot on the western edge of these mountains. I've packed as light as I could while still being prepared for what late September may throw at me up here, so my pack feels manageable. Each step makes me feel just a little bit lighter, even if they've all been uphill so far. It's a wonderful rhythm, punctuated by frequent visits with my water bottle, and occasional sit-down rests—to snack, and to jot down some of my hiking thoughts in my journal.

I'm now at Comanche Pass. I look back into the drainage that I spent the last several hours in. There isn't a cloud in the sky. The wind is consistent but relatively gentle as I notice the rich blue of Comanche Lake. I pull out my water bottle and take a long drink of cold filtered water from the lake. A part of the lake is now a part of me. Lodge? What Lodge? Ah, it's working!

North to Phantom Terrace, a trail carved into a gray cliff face that I hiked across once, several years ago, on a long day hike with a friend. Each step is taken much more deliberately, as the trail on the Terrace isn't as wide as I thought it was, but the drop off to my right is just as I remembered—straight down. The trail is entirely in the shade, so I watch for ice. A slip here and I will have traveled much farther away than I want to.

Safely across Phantom Terrace, a slow grind up and over 12,800' Venable Pass, and I am camped on the west side of the pass in a lonely lakeless basin surrounded by scratchy brown grasses and shrubby willows. Tent set up, enough water filtered to get me through the night and tomorrow morning, split pea soup dinner heartily consumed and cleaned up, and I am sitting outside the tent facing west, bundled in wool and fleece, warm despite a steady wind. A lovely pink-cloud sunset is today's "beautiful scene number ninety-seven" or so, with a V-shaped sliver of the San Luis Valley and the distant San Juan Mountains darkening quickly as this day ends. It's been a great day. I covered seven or eight miles today, most of it uphill. I am tired, really tired. But it's that good kind of tired after working—physically working—hard.

I now realize that it's been hours since I last thought of the Lodge and MPEC—work that I love but still need a break from. For me, it is wild Nature that gives me the best chance of walking away, physically, yes, but also mentally, and emotionally. "You don't go there to find something," Wallace Stegner once said of wilderness, "you go there to disappear." Disappear. Walking away. That's why I'm here, to disappear into this wildness for a few days, this "geography of hope," as Stegner calls it. So, the demands that could rob me of my sanity, don't. So, I can walk out of this wilderness in a few days, reassured of my own sanity, ready to continue the work that I love.

## People Need Nature
*November 2007*

All of these are related:

- According to the National Science Foundation, forty-five million Americans believe the oceans are a source of fresh water.
- Only 12% of Americans can pass a basic test on energy awareness.
- The Center for Disease Control reports that the number of overweight adult Americans increased over 60% between 1991 and 2000.
- Two out of every ten American children are clinically obese, four times the percentage of childhood obesity reported in the late 1960s.
- The average eight-year-old is able to identify numerous cartoon characters and even corporate logos, but cannot identify common plant or animal species found in his or her own neighborhood, such as an oak tree or a beetle.

These are all symptoms of a societal trend away from spending time in Nature. Author Richard Louv refers to it as "nature-deficit disorder' in his popular 2005 book, *Last Child in the Woods: Saving Our Children from Nature-Deficit Disorder.* Louv's intent was not to identify a new medical condition, but to capture in a phrase the human and community costs of our growing alienation from the natural world. "I like to play indoors 'cause that's where all the electrical outlets are," says a fourth grader quoted in Louv's book, illustrating a facet of this disconnect with Nature.

As director of a Nature education center, every day I see exactly what Louv and these agencies are talking about. Our children are truly "plugged in" (averaging 30 hours a week in front of a TV or computer monitor), with lives dominated by electronic gadgetry and mass media. Sadly, so many of today's children are in poor physical shape. Too many have no idea what it's like to build a dam in a stream, or be in a place where the sounds of cars cannot be heard. Our informal surveys indicate that a large majority of Pueblo's fifth graders (10- and 11-year-olds) have never gone on a hike and have never been to the mountains prior to participating in one of our programs—and they live 25 miles away from mountains.

Such lack of Nature experiences impacts both children's overall health as well as their attitudes towards the natural world. Although computers and the internet are a great tool (I use them every day), they are a poor substitute for experiencing first-hand the wonders of the natural world. And they are no substitute for what Moms everywhere used to say, "Go outside and play." Such a simple yet wise admonition. Recent research is proving just how wise it was. And still is!

The National Science Foundation believes that a citizenry with a fundamental understanding of the Earth's natural systems—an ecologically literate citizenry—is imperative if we are to successfully meet the many environmental challenges that are manifesting as the 21$^{st}$ century unfolds. Just as having a good working knowledge of numbers is required to balance a checkbook, a basic knowledge of, say, the water cycle, energy sources, and ecological concepts like carrying capacity are part of an ecological literacy that citizens will be called upon to have as our nation and our communities address these environmental challenges.

Pueblo County is projected to grow to 200,000 people by the year 2030, about 50,000 more people than today. Such growth will bring with it many decisions about the natural world. Should residential and commercial development be allowed everywhere, or should some areas be off-limits to development? If so, which ones, and why? What about wildlife populations? Should wildlife habitat be considered as our community grows? Do other species have intrinsic value beyond their utilitarian value to humans? What if we see no utilitarian value in a species' existence? What then? And water—is there enough? Should human use of water take precedence over aquatic species' need for minimum stream flows when shortages arise, as they surely will? These and others are all questions that require basic ecological literacy, of voters and leaders alike, if they are to be addressed wisely.

Nature-deficit disorder, and lack of literacy about the natural world, are community-wide problems, ones which begin in childhood. Their remedy, what Louv calls a "nature-child reunion," will require a community-wide effort to take an honest look at our communities' cultural patterns, involving many segments of our community.

If we want parents to say, "go outside and play," then our neighborhoods should provide safe access to natural settings, which is the business of community planners.

According to educator David Orr, the average high school graduate has spent 12,000 hours in a classroom. "All education is environmental education. By what is included and excluded, emphasized or ignored, students learn that they are a part of or apart from the natural world. Through all education we inculcate ideas of careful stewardship or carelessness." Hence, our schools have a vital role to play in the Nature-child reunion. Outdoor classrooms (simply a quiet area, maybe with some benches, under a large shade tree for hot days, in a sunny protected area for cooler days), partnerships with zoos and Nature centers, and sustainability projects (e.g. tree plantings, recycling programs, alternative energy projects) are a few of the countless ways that schools can be a part of the solution.

Health care practitioners can become familiar with the recent scientific research providing much evidence that direct exposure to Nature may be necessary for healthy childhood development. Studies indicate that ADHD, depression, and self-esteem (which are directly tied to choice-making around issues such as substance abuse and teen pregnancy) all respond positively to spending time in Nature. Armed with such knowledge, doctors can encourage outdoor time for their patients both young and not-so-young.

"What's important is that children have an opportunity to bond with the natural world, to learn to love it and feel comfortable in it, before being asked to heal its wounds." I believe these words by Antioch Professor David Sobel should be a guiding principle in developing a Nature-child reunion plan for any community.

The process of learning to love and feel comfortable with Nature, which means getting our children, and the rest of us, out in it, will be a huge step in the direction away from many health problems and their significant personal, financial and community costs. And, getting our children and ourselves outside will be a huge step in the direction of being literate about the natural world. Socrates said that knowledge begins with wonder. What better place to stimulate wonder—and knowledge, and healthy people—than the natural world!

**Finding Meaning in Beauty**
*December 3, 2007*

"The world is beautiful, in many unfathomable ways world is beautiful, in many unfathomable ways. In our hurrying, though, we frequently miss what is beautiful, in the same way that we forget from time to time what we want our lives to mean." I recently came across these two sentences in the latest issue of *National Geographic* from an essay on permafrost, written by Barry Lopez. It spoke of the impact of global warming on the frozen lands of our planet, and the impact on the planet of these lands becoming unfrozen. And it spoke of the beauty of these lands. The facts in the essay were interesting, the photographs were spectacular, but these two lines spoke to me.

I spent this morning completing various office tasks, crossing them off this week's new to-do list as I went along. On my walk back to the office after going home for lunch, with many more to-do's waiting for me, I remembered these lines. So, instead of jumping right back into the list, I've set off for an afternoon saunter to see some of the beauty that I've been missing.

No more than five minutes into the walk, I notice a pair of mule deer, well camouflaged against the wintry tones of the landscape. I quietly walk to within about 50 feet of them. The doe and her large fawn of last spring appear relaxed and not all that concerned with me. A casual glance would have them looking almost like twins, the juvenile just a bit smaller than its mother. But as I study them, I see that the younger one is quite a bit darker. Both are showing healthy winter coats, but the younger one's coat is much more brown, with less white under its neck. Where the adult's tail area is bright white, the smaller one's is more tan.

They begin to wander away. I resume walking and spy a fallen ponderosa snag. I go over to get a closer look at several large holes pecked into its now pulpy trunk. One has a large cavity just below a one-and-a-half-inch diameter hole. I wonder how many woodpeckers, chickadees, or nuthatches started their lives in there?

Now I'm examining a small deer antler that a young buck lost. I'm not the first to discover it. Many small teeth have been gnawing at it. In some places, it is nearly gnawed through. Dropped antlers are an important source of calcium for small mammals, and this shows lots of evidence of providing just that, so I leave it for the rodents.

I'm heading for a steep south-facing hillside just north of a drainage along the park's upper road. I figure I'll have about an hour of sunshine up there before the sun slides behind the ridge. I scramble up the loose scree and find an inviting place to sit against a crumbly piece of dull orange granite covered in many pale-green lichens. I settle into my sunny perch. A chickadee calls from the dense forest across the drainage. The reddish-brown soil seems to prefer growing small rocks, as there are lots of them. Several clumps of dried grasses sport prolific seeds. I recognize blue grama and little bluestem, a third species is mountain muhly, I think, and a fourth is beyond my knowledge of grasses. The yellow or reddish stems (bluestem has red stems—don't ask me why it's called bluestem) are moving ever so slightly in a breeze I cannot feel. A few small pines, a couple of dried asters, and some leafless oaks round out the obvious parts of my immediate surroundings.

In the couple of hours since I left the office, I see why Lopez refers to "what is beautiful" and "what we want our lives to mean" in the same sentence. "We must journey out," says Terry Tempest Williams, "so we might journey in." These small journeys out into Nature's simple beauty, like this afternoon saunter, serve as an antidote to the part of my life defined by to-do lists. But they are more than that. They also allow me opportunities to journey in, to look at my life against the bigger picture. Today, being out, I recognize a feeling that I feel more and more lately—that crossing things off to-do lists is becoming less and less satisfying.

For now, to-do lists are going to remain. I run a small, busy nonprofit—there are always lists of things that need doing. All these little tasks do add up to very worthy accomplishments, which bring much rich meaning to my life. But these journeys out also remind me that there is more to life than accomplishing things. There is much meaning in simply being out. There is much meaning in simply experiencing, and in not missing, what is beautiful.

## Spring Is Coming
*January 27, 2008*

After what seems like a couple of months of colder-than-average winter, the last couple of days have felt downright balmy. With the thermometer threatening to top 50F, the blue-sky sun calls me out of my Sunday home to the park's Tower Trail.

I walk on some soft wet snow, trudge through sloppy mud, keep myself upright on ice, and hike some nearly dry trail tread to a small stand of five-feet tall Gambel oak. I remove my pack and gulp some water. Then, just like I've been doing about this time for the last several years, I begin to carefully examine the ground beneath the oaks. The snow is melted away save for a few small slushy patches.

There's plenty to see: A flattened stalk of nodding onion with a heavy crop of black seeds still sitting in an intact umbel of dried flowers. Brown oak leaves of last year covering gray oak leaves of the year before. Acorn caps, black from moisture. Several clumps of golden aster, light brown and lifeless. Yellow, almost white, dried grasses. All are decaying remains of plants at various stages of cycling back into soil.

I slide my fingers up a stalk of fringed sagewort and smell its sweet fragrance on my fingertips. The sagewort has a few light green leaves emerging on its lower branches. The greening sagewort and a few blades of green grass hint of what's to come as the lengthening days of February and March usher in another spring.

Sometimes by this date, a few blossoms of *Claytonia rosea*, or spring beauty, the year's first wildflower, can be found here underneath this little stand of oak. But not this year. Not yet. I poke around and find several green, lance-shaped leaves and red stems of this hardy mid-winter bloomer hiding in the duff, but no buds. Since 1999 (when I began recording the dates of such things), the earliest I've found the first blossoms of spring beauty is January 19 (2005), and the latest is February 27 (2004). Last year, I found one lonely blossom on February 9. Many more soon followed. *C. rosea* blooms until around the end of May, when it and many other spring wildflowers, such as mountain bladderpod, dwarf daisy, and Nelson larkspur are replaced by summer blossoms like yarrow, aspen daisy, and scarlet paintbrush. But spring beauty starts it all.

If these warm sunny days continue, I predict there will be a few pinkish-white spring beauty blossoms to please the careful eyes of Tower Trail hikers within the next week. If the cold weather returns with more snow, it will only delay what is already set in motion. A few mild days to melt the snow and these little plants will be showing off their five-petal flowers with five bright pink stamens to any observant hiker. Pile up some deep white stuff from an Albuquerque low (a low-pressure system that moves across northern New Mexico and is notorious for bringing big snows to this part of southern Colorado) and the blossoms will patiently sit it out under the snow. Once it melts, the flowers will once again share their beauty with anyone willing to notice them as they hike this trail.

Even on this mid-winter day, these little leaves of *Claytonia rosea* say what I came to this particular stand of Gambel oak to hear—spring is coming!

## Is This Cool or What?
*April 6, 2008*

I silently slip past the trailhead and onto the trail the same way a very hungry person walks into her favorite restaurant, or a tired toddler falls into the arms of her mother. The words of John Muir come to mind, "Nature's peace will flow into you as sunshine flows into trees. The winds will blow their own freshness into you, and the storms their energy, while cares will drop off like autumn leaves." I couldn't agree more, Mr. Muir.

I'm heading for a sunny hillside a half mile up the Northridge Trail. I haven't been on Northridge for a while, so I walk across some lingering snow at the bottom of the Devil's Dribble drainage and take a right at the T. Wild Nature begins to envelop me. The woods are alive with the sounds of birds. I hear a spotted towhee's percussive song, repeating about every fifteen seconds. It reminds me of many early spring mornings waking up to the same sound in a particular redrock canyon of southeast Utah, a place that is special to me. I notice I'm smiling.

Except for many blooming spring beauties, spring seems to be unfolding rather slowly among the park's wildflowers. Just as this thought enters my mind, I casually glance to my left and see my first Pasqueflower of the season. I step off the trail into a grassy opening in the ponderosas for a closer look. The lavender petals (technically, they are petal-like sepals) have not yet fully opened to reveal the flower's busy yellow center.

I hike up a red dirt section of trail. Several years ago, I spotted that year's first bear sign right here, a perfect five-toed track, indicating that our neighborhood bears had awakened from their winter's slumber. Any day now, I'll find a track, or a scat, or a bear itself, saying that hibernation is over for *Ursus americanus* this year.

I arrive at my hillside destination and find a downed log to sit against. A startled lizard scurries away as I get comfortable. The sun feels warm on this still-cool morning. I hear nothing but non-human sounds. Another towhee song. Dried grasses and oak leaves rattling in the breeze. Several chickadees calling. The squawk of a Steller's jay. The squeak of a woodpecker. A stronger breeze humming through the tall trees down the hill behind me. A towhee, this time not its song but its call that sounds a bit like a screaming monkey (at least according to fifth grade students I've worked with). The nasal *honk* of a red-breasted nuthatch.

The wildness of this place is further revealed by the view right in front of me. The farthest ridge still boasts lots of white snow along with the green of countless conifers. A few bands of gray just below a saddle are aspen trees, still leafless in their winter mode. Closer in are the crumbling (geologically speaking) granite rocks that make up Devil's Canyon, a few patches of snow saying that spring is still young. My eye catches some movement off to my right. A small raptor with an obvious white rump (northern harrier, I think) gracefully glides low over the naked shrubs and disappears into some trees.

To borrow a phrase that my four-year-old grandson Jude said several times yesterday, on his first fully self-powered hike to the Fire Tower, "Is this cool or what?" We tasted sprigs of emerging textile onion, were surprised by, and then sat and watched a beautiful 18-inch green snake ("It's my favorite color," said Jude, "light green."), climbed to the windy top of the tower three times, and ate our lunch in the warm sun—a perfect place for a boy and his grandpa to enjoy Nature, and each other. To think this Mountain Park, with thousands of acres of wild federal lands just behind it, is right here for all of us to experience wild Nature, and for Nature to carry on its wild ways—you are so right, little Ranger Jude, this place is cool!

## Creating Memories
*May 29, 2008*

As I approach the top of a short steep hill, dappled in shade from many young ponderosa pines, the sunny expanse of the meadow just east of the Devil's Canyon Trailhead opens before me. A hot wind dances with acres of six-inch-tall grass. The air moves not in a clean sweep, but in many seemingly independent waves of wind, clearly visible as one section of grass bends this way, another bends that way. It's like a visual symphony—blades of grass in each section play with the sun's light differently at any given moment.

I walk out into the windy meadow, as green as Ireland. The last time I was in this meadow, a few months ago, I was gliding about a foot above it, suspended by pure white snow, a pair of cross-country skis my happy mode of transport. I remember it well—a storm had just moved out, the sky was clearing as a short winter day neared its end, and a crisp twilight tinted with pink beckoned me to put an hour's delay on dinner with an after-work ski. How could I refuse! It was a delightful ski, and now part my long list of memories of being in this park.

As I walk along the Devil's Canyon Trail, other memories are sparked. Right here a few summers ago, at the bottom of the first hill, I introduced my grandson Jude to the sweet rewards of searching for tiny wild strawberries. If I take a right at this T in the trail, it leads to a meadow/forest ecotone where I've watched countless students discover the joys of sitting quietly in a natural place with a pair of binoculars. Now I am at the spot where Helene and I stopped short as our dog Lucy, exploring ahead of us as we hiked, startled a sleeping bear one July afternoon ten or so years ago. In less than the time it took me to say "Oh, shoot," or something like it, Lucy strategically placed herself safely behind us, barking many brave barks, Helene and I between her and the fleeing bear. The bear had no interest in hanging around as we watched his huge rump disappearing up the hill.

If I took the time, I could come up with hundreds of memories associated with this park. I have no doubt that this park is truly, literally, a part of me, as much a part of me as the water I just drank and the almonds I just ate. If you could remove this park and all its memories from me, it would be no stretch at all to say I would not be the same person.

Some cultures take this concept of the land being a part of themselves to the point of actually seeing the environment as an extension of their own selves, emphasizing the connections with the natural world and de-emphasizing the separateness of their bodies with their surroundings. I once heard environmental educator and author Joseph Cornell illustrate this sense of being a part of the natural world with this little anecdote: When children are asked to draw themselves, Navajo children draw themselves smaller, and also draw trees, clouds, plants, animals, other people—and call the entire drawing themselves. In contrast, non-native American children often take up the whole page to draw just their own body and call it themselves.

Beyond the poetic nature of all of this, I believe there is much wisdom in the belief that the self doesn't stop at the skin. The biology part of it is clear—the same raw materials (e.g. oxygen, carbon) endlessly cycle in and out of all living things and natural systems. If we see what is around us as an extension of our own selves, then protecting the plants and water and air—the Earth— is no different than protecting our own selves. I think such a belief could go a long way towards solving many of the environmental challenges we now face. How do we foster such a belief? A good place to start would be getting ourselves, and our children, out in Nature, creating memories.

## Playing it Safe with a Summer Thunderstorm
*July 28, 2008*

Flash! Crack! They're getting closer as I approach a more open section of the trail. Against my better judgment, I left the office twenty minutes ago to walk off a mind cluttered with way too many things. A quick-paced hike, I thought, is just what I need: get the heart pumping, blood flowing and lungs working while laying my eyes on trees, wildflowers, animal tracks—anything but the inside of my office. I heard some distant rumbles as I was filling my water bottle. Ah, it'll pass, I thought. Besides, the storm did seem a bit too far south to do anything more than brush the park with its edge. It's been doing that a lot lately.

Well, it's working. I'm not thinking about grants, budgets, programs, or policies. I am thinking about not getting fried by ten million volts of electricity. CRACK! Alright, with better judgment setting in, a few hundred yards up the Mace Trail, I turn around. I head back towards my MPEC office as the plunk and plink of raindrops hitting oak leaves and grass blades are added to the music of an emerging summer storm.

I find a comfortable spot to sit just off the road under a short, dense white fir tree in a stand of taller trees of similar heights, considered a relatively safe place to be when out in the backcountry in a thunderstorm. I'm still not convinced this storm will—FLASH/CRACK (at just about the same moment). OK, OK, I'm convinced—I'm heading back inside. Walking rather quickly, with the rain beginning to get more serious, I think: If I were in the backcountry now, I would get out my rain gear and hunker down like I've done so many times before, but I may as well play it safe.

Back under a roof, I open some windows and park myself so I can watch the storm. A cool breeze tempts me to leave my safe and dry spot, but I stay put. The sporadic raindrops of a little while ago have become, if not sheets of rain, a decent downpour. I love summer thunderstorms.

The storm peaks and is now nothing more than lots of rumbling steadily decreasing in volume. The rain outside the window has become light and gentle. Time to resume my walk. I step outside and one breath of moist, cool, post-rain mountain air fills me, invigorates me, soothes me. I'm amazed at how such a short summer rain can release such a delicious, sweet, rich smell. If I could taste this wonderful aroma, it would be a perfect green salad, a nutritious and healthy entree, and a delectable, sweet dessert all in one. All my senses now seem more alive.

Realizing I left my hat under the white fir tree I tried to ride out the storm under, I head in that direction. I notice one, then dozens of nodding onions, just beginning to bloom. The yellow of several pale goldenrods catches my eye, and many stiff goldenrods appear just about ready to bloom. I know they were all here earlier, but I just wasn't seeing them.

I reach the tree and find a soggy hat—the tree would have

offered less protection than I imagined. Instead of heading for the trail, I decide to check out the rain gauge. The road is muddy in places, with puddles here and there. My hunch is more rain fell than I thought while holed up dry and safe inside. The rain gauge reads 0.31 inches—certainly not a large rain, but more than I would have guessed from my spectator seat.

The drips from the trees are accompanied by a soft lingering rainfall. The lightning and thunder are now a distant whisper, so I think I'll walk some more and enjoy this needed respite from all those things that were cluttering up my head a short while ago. Boy, it sure smells good out here.

## Why a Nature Lover is Fixing Up an Old Building
*October 1, 2008*

A deep breath fills my lungs with cool, moist air that smells of the light rain that is very gently falling. I hear nothing but the busy calls of a bunch of pygmy nuthatches high in the tall ponderosa pines and droplets of water from the roof hitting the ground.

As I settle into my spot on the porch of the Lodge, sitting still and quiet, the wild creatures whose home is this park begin to present themselves. The blue of a western bluebird flying across the Lodge's front yard catches my eye. I look over towards the Pavilion and watch a doe and two healthy-sized fawns grazing on the grass. I hear scratches on the tree just off the porch, then watch its source appear as a white-breasted nuthatch scrambles straight down the tree's trunk. A black Abert's squirrel runs across the top of the Lodge's opposite wing. It hops onto the porch roof and a magpie lands right where the squirrel was moments before.

Reading through my last journal reveals that it was two years ago this week that I sat on this same porch, my back against this same adobe wall, reflecting on the Lodge renovation project that I was about to kick off. I am here to reflect some more. The last two years of my life have been filled with this project: fundraising, countless conversations, architects and engineers and contractors, budgets, updated budgets, weekends working with volunteers doing all sorts of jobs (demolition of old walls and painting of new walls stand out), and hours and hours at all times of the day or night planning, thinking, worrying, or scheming about a thousand decisions of all sorts... And, here I sit, my new office and a whole new MPEC headquarters are now inside these adobe walls. I've come such a long way in two years, yet I find myself wondering, "Why am I, a wild Nature advocate at heart, spending such a good chunk of my life fixing up an old building?"

More than anything, I love wild Nature—being out in it, teaching about it, learning about it, advocating for it. So, why the Lodge? I look up and notice that the dominant feature of where I am is a ponderosa pine forest. The Lodge, with its walls made of mud and straw, its log beams and posts made from locally-harvested trees, its simple lines and low profile tucked underneath these tall, storied pines—it is no stretch at all to see how this structure grew right out of this land, with wild creatures living their lives all around it.

Knowing its history—that this park and this Lodge grew out of an idea that our nation's citizens should get out into our nation's forests—the answer to my question is clear. The Lodge was constructed in the 1930s to facilitate people using our wild forests for recreation and learning, as envisioned by another wilderness advocate, Arthur Carhart. All I'm doing is taking Carhart's vision, and the Lodge, which has seen so little use the last few decades, and updating its 1930s style into a facility appropriate for today, and for many, many years to come— sort of like midwifing the rebirth of the Horseshoe Lodge. The Lodge will once again be a "base camp," a place from which people can go out and explore, enjoy and experience wild Nature, just as Carhart envisioned.

I've always said that it is hard to get people to advocate for wild Nature if they've never experienced it. With so many distractions, people are spending less and less time in Nature, resulting in a kind of Nature-deficit disorder, as author Richard Louv refers to it. It feels good to know that all of my work on the Lodge is still wilderness advocacy, as the Lodge will facilitate the human-Nature connection, and ultimately create more citizen advocates for wild Nature.

## Reading the Stories in the Snow
*November 2008*

The last several days have brought a couple inches of snow, finally bringing the landscape a bit closer to matching the calendar. The thin layer of snow also reveals the presence of our animal neighbors as they quietly do their thing, often unnoticed yet right under our noses. Tracking animals is made so much easier by winter's snow, and the first few storms of the season remind me of the additional pleasure that observing animal tracks brings to my winter forays into the natural world.

I noticed several delicate, four-toed tracks on my walk to the office this morning. A closer inspection showed subtle claw marks in front of the roughly two-inch-wide and two-and-a half-inch-long tracks. I've learned that the pattern of tracks (their relationship to one another) is at least as revealing as the features of an individual track itself. These tracks appeared to be almost in a straight line, about 15" apart. A red fox, walking. *Vulpes vulpes* often walks by placing its rear foot directly in the place where the front foot just was, known as "direct register." Each track I saw in the snow was actually two tracks, one directly on top of the other. The fox also tends to keep its feet underneath the center of its body—hence, the tracks in a line.

There was also regularity to the tracks, with a certain deliberate and careful placement of the feet obvious in the tracks. This fox was out on a chilly wintry night, and it didn't just have a bowl of dog food, fed to it by its owner. It most probably had food on its mind—food that it would have to successfully hunt first. If the front foot landed quietly, no sense in taking the chance of scaring a potential meal by placing the rear foot on a branch that might snap. For comparison, a domestic dog's walking pattern is usually much sloppier, moving here and there with much less care than a fox. A dog's walking track pattern usually double- or indirect-registers, with its rear foot next to or partially on top of the front foot placement.

Another common set of tracks in the area comes in a cluster of four individual tracks. The Abert's squirrel (the black squirrel with tufts of hair on its ears, seen among ponderosa pines) moves by bounding, so the track pattern has the smaller front feet tracks registering *behind* the larger rear feet tracks relative to the direction of travel. When bounding, *Sciurus aberti's* front feet hit the ground first, with the rear feet landing in front of where the front feet landed. If conditions are good, you can see four toes on the front feet and five on the back, with claws sometimes registering in very good tracking conditions (like a thin snow cover). The clusters of tracks can be as much as three feet apart, and if you follow them, you'll see that they usually start at the bottom of one tree and end at the bottom of another.

Yes, winter brings with it several ways to enjoy a simple walk in the park: the brilliant blue sky on a crisp sunny day, the magic of the first snowflakes of a just-getting-started winter storm, and stories in the tracks of some of the wild creatures we share the neighborhood with.

**That Place Where I Know Exactly Who I Am**
*December 10, 2008*

I forgot what a workout breaking trail, uphill, on snowshoes is. Yesterday's 14 inches of fresh snow, now wet and heavy as the morning matures, only adds to the workout. Each step takes me farther away from the Center, where a few dozen fifth graders from Pueblo are getting their first feel of walking through snow with these weird contraptions strapped to their feet.

Before I left on my solo hike, I helped MPEC's teachers strap snowshoes onto a bunch of those feet. "Excitement" is certainly the word that captures the mood of these students. But I heard some "I'm scared," "I'm nervous," "I hope I can do this" comments as well. Our surveys of a few years ago told us that over 60% of the ten- and eleven-year-olds that we work with have never been on a hike prior to an MPEC program. Well, it became obvious while I was helping out that 100% of today's students have never been on snowshoes. Not anymore—now 100% can say they have snowshoed!

Many seeds of a lifetime of healthful outdoor winter recreation are being planted today. I send a good thought out into this lovely blue sky that every seed grows into a strong plant, firmly rooted in a love for being outdoors.

Each step also takes me a little deeper into the less-peopled part of the park, admittedly where I need to be for a little while today. After some good walking, I find a sunny rock, sweep off most of the snow, and plant myself on it. I breathe, look, and listen. The trees are steadily losing their snow in countless drips, punctuated every now and then by a loud plop as a large clump slides off a branch. A chickadee is calling from way off in front of me, while the high-pitched call of a Townsend's solitaire comes from behind. The sun is low in a sky that is too blue to believe. This couldn't be a more perfect place to be.

At this moment, I hear no human-made sounds. I hiked to the more remote part of the park because my own sense of rootedness needs a recharge. Rooted, grounded, connected, belonging—known as *querencia* in Spanish, according to an article I recently read. The author quoted Barry Lopez to further define the word as "a place on the ground where one feels secure, a place from which one's strength of character is drawn—a place in which we know exactly who we are."

The many hats I wear running MPEC have me wondering just who I am lately. As MPEC's growth seems to demand more and more of me, I feel less and less sure of my own sense of *querencia*. And that's why I am here, because this part of the park is that "place on the ground" where things become clear: that place where I can feel rooted once again.

I've only been out a couple of hours, and while I know I am going to need regular doses of this kind of medicine to regain that sense of connection I seek, I can feel that it is working. At the risk of sounding like a cliché, every time I choose to just walk away from it all for a little while, I am the better for it—as if the dark sunglasses are removed, and I can more clearly see who I am.

Enos Mills, known as the "Father of Rocky Mountain National Park," a well-rooted person who spent much time alone in the wilderness, wrote: "The trail compels you to know yourself and to be yourself, and puts you in harmony with the universe. It makes you glad to be living. It gives health, hope, and courage, and it extends that touch of nature which tends to make you kind." I can tell you that, right now, I know why he wrote those words. Because they are true.

## I Choose it All
*March 4, 2009*

It is one of those days that, for me, is hard to love. The sky is blue and the sun is welcoming as I hike up the Mace Trail, but an in-my-face, way-too-warm-for-March 4 wind blasting across a bone-dry landscape steals most of my focus, hard as I try to not let it. Despite a few pretty spring beauty blossoms here and there, each powerful gust seems to scream *drought* across the brown, snowless ground.

This morning I tallied the park's February snow totals. It didn't take long—2.3 inches. Last night's news told me about a 6,500-acre fire south of Colorado Springs and, crazily, a 40-plus-acre fire near Florissant. Florissant is over 8,000' in altitude! How can a wildfire be burning at that altitude, on March 3? March is supposed to be this part of Colorado's snowiest month. What's going on?

Yes, I admit it, strong dry winds coupled with a parched snowless March landscape around my mountain home is a challenge to my serenity.

I look down and spot a dried, curled scat. A fox has been here! The scatologist in me finds a rock—I break apart the scat with it. A small jawbone, no longer than a centimeter, falls out of the scat's tightly packed gray hairs. I closely examine the tiny set of teeth. Cool! A switch has flipped inside of me. My despair over the drought and wind fades a bit as I am cognizant of a magical sense of wonder waking inside of me.

The predator-prey dance between the fox and rodent revealed in the scat now plays in my head. OK, it is dry and windy. No, it hasn't snowed much. But foxes continue to hunt, right here in this drought-stricken landscape—proof that, drought and all, Nature's rhythms continue. A loud, powerful gust reminds me that the wind is still here, along with foxes and field mice and kangaroo rats and so much more to be discovered, if I only keep looking.

Author Sharman Apt Russell shares this piece of wisdom:

> I have learned (somewhat slowly) that if I want to have a relationship with the natural world, it can't just be with the parts I pick and choose. The gorgeous mountain view makes my lover's heart ache. But I also ... have to get to know the parts of nature that make me wince and turn away. Because turning away is not really what good lovers do.

Russell is right; I can't pick and choose only the parts I like and still be a good lover—of Nature, or anyone or anything else. So, I choose it all: my delight in discovering that tiny jawbone; my fearful pause as a wildly strong gust of wind stops a breath in my chest, half expecting some branch to come flying out of a tree at me (it doesn't); sunshine reflecting off a million pine needles dancing in the wind; a plume of dust lifting off a section of trail. Drought. Wonder. Wind. Calm. Hot. Cold. Life. Death. Nature's upbeats and downbeats. For better and for worse.

Come on, wind, take my hand and hike with me along this sunny, fox-traveled trail. Who knows what we might discover around the next dusty bend?

**What is Normal?**
*June 7, 2009*

An hour ago, this cool, partly cloudy day became gray and windy. Now, as I head out for an easy afternoon saunter, the sky is nearly cloudless blue, the breeze gentle, and the sunshine is as warm and welcoming as a woodstove on a cold winter day. It's as if this day is saying, "Cold weather is over, and summer is about to make its entrance."

While the day is talking summer, the land is shouting *green*. A photosynthesis party is in high gear, thanks to a very wet spring. The green is punctuated by other bright colors: the orange of western wallflower, purple-blue of low penstemon, yellow of Fendler senecio, pink of textile onion. I hear a hoarse *bird-ie* and look up to see the striking yellow, black and orange of a western tanager fly by a few feet in front of me. But it is still green that dominates the landscape—light green, dark green, blue green, almost black-shaded green, green with a touch of yellow, soft green. The word green, by itself, doesn't come close to capturing the diversity of color, the numerous shades and textures that are spread out all around me. It is like using the word *beautiful* to describe Beethoven's Ninth Symphony. "Beautiful" just doesn't touch the depth, the richness, the passion, the countless ways of experiencing such a musical masterpiece.

I never would have predicted such a prolific riot of green when winter officially ended several weeks ago. Up to the spring equinox, the park saw less than 50 inches of snow. By the season's final April 18 snowfall, winter 2009 went into the record books with 83.5 inches of snow, 73% of the "normal" 115 inches. May's 4.3 inches of rain turned it all around.

*Normal.* Now there's another word that needs some exploration. The meteorological definition is "the arithmetic mean over a 30-year period." Or, more simply, the 30-year average. Now, to me, the word *normal*, when used in this context, says that $x$ amount of moisture is where we "should be" (a phrase commonly used by meteorologists) by such and such a date. It implies, at least to my ear, that anything above or below that amount is, by default, abnormal. So, is 83.5 inches of winter snow abnormal? Not according to historical precipitation records. It is certainly below the recent 30-year average, below where meteorologists say we "should be." But it is not abnormal.

Use of such language seems to ignore natural climate variability. The last 30 years of winter snow totals in the park included 83.5 inches (2009), 93 inches (1999) and 75 inches (2001), as well as 128 inches (1995), 149 inches (1994) and 141 inches (2004). They may be drier or wetter than average snow seasons, but they are not abnormal. When these, along with all the other snow totals of the last 30 years are averaged, the result is the mythical "normal" that we hear weather reporters refer to. If anything, a snow season that exactly matches the "normal" amount of snow is rather unusual, or abnormal. It is like saying that a normal American man "should be" 5 feet 10 inches tall. What about all us guys who are 5 feet 7 inches, or 6 feet 2 inches—are we abnormal? Of course not. Five feet 10 inches is the average, and not what a guy should be.

This all may sound like hair-splitting, but I think there is a real danger in using such language for moisture amounts, particularly in places like Colorado, where, according to precipitation records between 1893 and 1996, 33 of those years were "dry" years. This "normal" and "should be" language gives the impression that a dry year is unusual, and we'll soon get back to normal (read: wet). Such impressions translate into Kentucky bluegrass lawns, limitless development, and unsustainable consumption of water. The reality is, dry/drought years are far from unusual in Colorado. In fact, we should expect them, because they are quite normal around here. Factor in how the changing climate is exacerbating these dry years, and below average snow years are becoming even more common.

I look up to see a reddish bird fly by, landing at the top of a Douglas fir. Binoculars reveal a red crossbill. Nice! This is a bird that is seen in the park some years, and not seen at all other years. It looks like this year is a crossbill year! Last summer wasn't. Its presence or absence are both "normal" for the park. Just like snowfall—some years there's a lot of it, some years not that much. Such variations are perfectly normal!

## It's Just Me and the Birds
*August 22, 2009*

I step out the front door with a handful of almonds at 5:59 a.m., intent on experiencing some solitude while I witness the day's first rays of sunshine finding their way onto the hilly terrain of the Mountain Park. The air is milder than I expected. Several noisy ravens are the first sounds that I hear. Other birds are busy and vocal as I add my gravelly footsteps to the summer morning: the *chick-a-dee-dee-dee* of mountain chickadees, the high-pitched chatter of pygmy nuthatches, the whistle of a male broad-tailed hummingbird (only the male broad-tailed whistles as it flies, not the female).

I turn the corner into the park and the faint but unmistakable whiff of a skunk helps wake me up. A two-note phrase of a bird I don't recognize adds to the morning mix. Up the dirt road I walk.

Quick steps and I am soon on the soft tread of the Tower Trail. Up the trail I hike until I find a welcoming spot among the oaks with a clear view to the east and sit myself down. A raucous pair of flickers land on a snag to my right, as if to say, "Hey, we're joining you. You have a problem with that?" The few thin clouds in the eastern sky are already bright orange. It won't be long now. Just before the sun itself begins to peak over the ridge, what sounds like a whole choir of chickadees and nuthatches lets loose a wild cacophony of sound. It's like they are saying, "Without further ado, we give to you—The Sun!" And with that, the upper edge of a late summer sun begins to slip into view.

The solar point of rising is much further south than it was a couple months ago. Although still a hot summer sun, I've been noticing over the last week or so how its light looks somehow different. Our part of the Earth's tilt is migrating away from the sun, and it is beginning to show in longer shadows and a light that seems softer. The changing light, the dried yarrow heads, the prolific number of asters and late summer daisies, the yellowing grasses with heavy seeds weighing them down—all clearly say that summer will soon be on its way out, with autumn right on its tail.

Some movement in the oaks right in front of me eventually reveals a scruffy looking spotted towhee, a juvenile born earlier this summer. I wonder if it knows that these hot summer days will soon be replaced by cool autumn days, and then short, cold winter days. I choose not to tell him—he'll find out soon enough. The bird sounds do not diminish as the sun climbs further above the ridge.

Solitude. One definition says that solitude is "Time alone, in quiet, with no noise save the noise of the natural breathing, which comes from a centered Earth." I would venture to say that all this chatter of birds is a perfect example of the Earth's natural breathing.

This early morning, it's just me and the birds, watching a late summer sunrise. Good morning, sun, welcome to a new day! And the birds just keep on chattering.

## Pueblo's Best Idea
*December 2, 2009*

A small gust brings a hint of whiteout to a crisp, snowy morning hike. After several wet autumn snows, today finally feels like winter. Each step releases a crunchy squeak as the dry powder compresses under my weight. Additional strong bursts of wind subtract from the visibility as I hike up the Tower Trail. Tracks of deer and squirrels tell me I am not alone out here.

I arrive at my destination—a dense stand of Douglas fir trees on a north-facing slope halfway up the trail. I find a somewhat protected place under a cluster of trees to sit, pull out my journal and a water bottle, and here I am. The snow reaching the page, temps in the low teens, and continuing gusts of wind may make this spot seem to be a less than ideal place to write. So it may seem, but it's exactly where I want to be.

You see, I sat in this very place over a dozen years ago, on the same kind of cold snowy day as today, and wrote in my journal. I remember well sitting right here that day, listening to snowflakes landing on my jacket, an occasional bird, and not much else. I remember writing that day about my love for this park, and for Nature. I wrote on that cold day about what I could do with that love, and where that love might lead. It was moments like that one, sitting right here with my journal, and hiking alone along these trails, where the idea of creating MPEC was born. It was moments like that one that kept me going as I dealt with one hurdle after another to make the idea of MPEC a reality. And it continues to be these moments, these solo walks in this park, that keep me going as I'm about to enter MPEC's second decade.

I thought I'd come up here to write this essay several evenings ago, while watching the Ken Burns documentary *The National Parks: America's Best Idea*. The film, all about the love of parks, somehow made me think of sitting and writing right here, under these trees, like I did several years ago. So, I scheduled Wednesday morning, December 2, for a "walk and write," as I refer to these reflective saunters of mine. That the weather turns out to be identical with the wintry weather all those years ago, when I sat right here, makes this moment only more perfect. I can think of no place I'd rather be.

Watching Ken Burns' film was like a religious experience for me. No, Pueblo Mountain Park is not a Yellowstone, a Yosemite, a Rocky Mountain National Park. It is only a small local Mountain Park, so humble in comparison to the majestic grandeur of all those spectacular places. And, although I am but a small part of the evolution of this Mountain Park, I found myself relating to the stories, the dreams, the tireless efforts of our National Parks' champions. These people are my heroes. If it wasn't for John Muir, and Stephen Mather, and Enos Mills, and, in the case of Pueblo Mountain Park, Arthur Carhart, and so many others, all these parks that are so important to our nation, to so many people, and to me, would probably not exist. And neither would MPEC.

As I watched the film, I could see so many parallels between those grand places and this Mountain Park. Any place where Nature can be found "with all its complexity and abundance of life," may be, as biologist George Melendez Wright said, America's "greatest national heritage." Any place that has been set aside to give people the opportunity to be a part of Nature—just as I am experiencing right now, right here in this little Mountain Park—is what makes these places America's best idea. So, I officially proclaim from this snowy, tree-covered hillside that Pueblo Mountain Park is Pueblo's Best Idea.

My hands are cold. The wind and snow continue. It is time to resume my hike. I look up to see my pack covered in countless large snowflakes, each one a perfect and unique six-armed star. I am so glad I am here, in this park that I so love. This has been the perfect place for me to sit, think, and write—and now this trail is the perfect place to continue my winter morning saunter and be a part of Nature.

**I Just Can't Wait**
*February 20, 2010*

I pour melted snow into the measuring tube: point two one. The first day of this stingy February storm brought 2.8" of snow, now melted and measuring twenty-one hundredths of an inch of moisture. A snowy yesterday evening is now followed by a gray dreary day.

Ignoring the voice inside of me that earlier said, "Stay home, relax, finish that book, it looks nasty out there," I layered up for a morning hike. My detour to measure and record the precipitation complete, I arrive at the trailhead of the Mace Trail. Most of the nearby meadow has been lost to a thick fog. No grand vistas on this hike.

I notice the bare branches of an oak with crystal spikes that look exactly like white thorns, compliments of twenty-two degrees and one hundred percent humidity. Some are nearly an inch long. Further snooping reveals many different forms of ice crystals. The spikes on the ponderosa needles aren't as long as the ones on the oaks. I find a line of crystals floating beneath the needles of a Douglas fir branch, clinging to an invisible strand of spider web. Nature's small but magical works of art will apparently be my focus on today's hike.

I hear a tiny sound I believe may be from a golden-crowned kinglet, a small bird I don't often see. I decide to see if its curiosity will bring it in closer: *psshhh, psshhh, psshhh, psshhh!* No kinglet, but out of nowhere come a couple of curious mountain chickadees. I can see a slight tinge of rust on their sides, adding just a bit of color to their black, white and gray. More *psshhh's* soon have a couple dozen busy little birds flitting all around me, their curiosity getting the better of them. Along with the chickadees are a few red-breasted nuthatches, always the most curious. One works its way within a couple feet of my face. Ignoring my drippy nose, I stand perfectly still and enjoy feeling like the Pied Piper of little birds. A lone pygmy nuthatch, smaller but much louder than the others, is making a racket just above my head. I slowly move my gaze straight up and see it, clinging to the trunk of a skinny ponderosa.

I stop at a point along the trail where I usually look out across the valley to the hillside where my house sits, with the plains and Pueblo behind it. Beyond the shrubs directly in front of me, all I can see are a few frosted pines that look like tree ghosts floating in foggy nothingness. The rest of the landscape has simply vanished.

I am now past the high point of today's hike, descending through a dense stand of Douglas fir and white fir trees. Signs in the snow tell me that several squirrels have been working their way between trees. I find a perfect four-toed track made by the delicate foot of a pine squirrel, a common resident of these stands. Now out of the trees and again walking among the oaks, I notice the tracks of another rodent, but one I don't usually see.

They look like mouse tracks, with the tail dragging, but with huge rear feet. Kangaroo rat! The tracks climb into a cluster of leafless shrubs and disappear in some deep snow.

I am glad I didn't listen to that voice that told me to stay home. I would have missed so many little natural delights that can only be discovered by going out on an icy, dreary day like today. The runner's tracks I followed while ascending the trail revealed that I am not the only person who decided to venture out along this trail today. This person, who by the looks of the tracks was a couple of hours ahead of me, took pretty short steps on the uphill. But downhill, the wide distance between the tracks tells me he or she was cruising.

Snooping around for little natural wonders, getting a workout on a trail run—two perfectly good reasons to throw on the woolies, lace up the boots, and get outside, even on a bleak late February day.

As I near the end of the trail, I get to where, just a week ago, I showed a group of hikers a couple of blooming spring beauties, small pink and white wildflowers growing on plants no more than two or three inches tall. Wait until warm spring days to bloom? Hardly! It may still be winter, but these flowers just couldn't wait to get on with life. I can relate. And, I bet, so would that trail runner.

**A Sacred Place**
*May 31, 2010*

The extra shirt I put on as I began this morning hike is now stashed in my pack. The lingering cool of the night is no match for the sun climbing into a cloudless sky so blue I can scarcely believe it is real. The sky ends at the mountainous horizon drawn with the tops of thousands of conifers. I've been looking at this same tree-lined horizon for nearly thirty-five years, but this morning it is like I'm seeing it for the first time.

When I left my house an hour ago, I didn't know where in the park I would wind up. As I made my way along the park's roads, this south-facing hillside a little way up the Northridge Trail whispered my name—not the first time it has done so, as this is a frequent sitting spot of mine. And now here I sit, comfortably situated on the gravelly soil, melting into the beauty of where I am. "This world is so beautiful I can hardly believe it exists." Ralph Waldo Emerson must have been in a setting like this when he wrote those words.

I bring my attention to the land within a dozen or so feet of where I sit. There are several small yuccas, a few with a stalk of chocolate-brown flower buds, just a few days from opening. The mountain mahogany is covered in yellowish-white horn-shaped blossoms. The fading yellow blossoms of several mountain bladderpod are well past their prime. The bright violet-blue of many low penstemon, in contrast, appears fresh and vibrantly alive, standing out amongst the many shades of green that dominate the scene.

The audible landscape provides a perfect avian soundtrack to all that I see. The bird-chorus includes: the whistles of broad-tailed hummingbirds zipping by; the familiar melodies of several American robins; a few black-headed grosbeaks, who sound like robins in exceptionally good voice; the relatively unmelodic song of a western wood peewee; the basso-continuum of a mourning dove's lamenting *coo-oo* along with the percussive trill of several spotted towhees; the metallic-sounding songs of dark-eyed juncos; the call of a dusky flycatcher that ends in a small ascending interval (a minor third if my ear is working properly); the loud squawk of a hairy woodpecker; the buzz of a tiny blue-gray gnatcatcher.

A movement on the left catches my eye. A small lizard is doing push-ups on a silver sun-bleached log. A bird flying by grabs my attention. It lands on an upper branch of a ponderosa—the striking tropical red and bright yellow of a western tanager, recently arrived from Central America. Can it get any better than this?

I have been in New York City's beautiful St. Patrick's Cathedral and the magnificent Air Force Academy Chapel. I've been in scores of churches and temples and places of worship all around the country. For me, none of those places can match the peace, the tranquility, the sense that I am in a sacred place that I am experiencing right here. The words of Henry David Thoreau—another transcendentalist and a friend of Emerson—capture just what I am feeling right now, "Heaven is under our feet as well as over our heads." Or, to localize Mr. Thoreau's sentiments, Heaven is this south-facing hillside on this late spring morning.

## The Wind is Talking, and I am Listening
*August 30, 2010*

It's happening again. I can tell by what is blooming—golden aster, Kansas gayfeather, sunspots, rough white aster, stiff goldenrod, western mugwort (an *Artemisia*, which leaves a glorious earthy aroma on my fingers when I slide them across its unassuming flower heads). I can tell by the birds' relative quiet at dawn. The sunlight itself seems different. Along with arriving a bit later and departing a bit earlier each day, its illumination of the land is somehow different than it was in June when the summer was young. Maybe it's the sun's lower position in the sky, but to my eye the light itself seems to have taken on a subtle yellow tint, as if wanting to enhance the upcoming coloring of the landscape as leaves begin to turn.

I can tell by the wind, which is whispering, "A change is coming" to anyone who slows down enough to listen. I can tell by how quickly the air cools in the evening, and by how I almost wished I had a jacket on my walk to the park this morning.

Even if everyone in my life somehow conspired to trick me by turning every calendar I encounter to read May, or June, or even July, I would not be fooled. Autumn is fast on its way, summer is about done, and everything around me tells me this is so.

The natural world is a busy place in summer. The long hot days are for the business of life. Everything is growing, expanding, moving, reproducing. Everything is fully alive. But that busy time of summer lasts only so long, and the landscape now says it clearly—summer is about over as it is all beginning to slow down. Autumn is when the natural world manifests the bounty of the summer season, like the fat acorns I've been seeing on the Gambel oaks. It took the whole summer for the land to grow those acorns out of last spring's little oak flowers.

I can also tell that autumn is coming by what I am noticing in my inner landscape. It has been a busy, mobile and productive summer for me too, and the voice inside of me is clearly saying it is time for me to slow down as well. Slowing down my own pace in the fall creates the space to reflect on what I might harvest from my own summer busyness.

Not that making this shift comes easy. There is something self-perpetuating about being so busy—summer is fun, alive, invigorating—and there certainly is a part of me that doesn't want to see it end. But I take all those changes in the natural landscape—the late summer flowers, the changing light, the cooler mornings and evenings—as my cue to begin moving out of my summer patterns and begin the process of slowing down.

So here I am, on a deliberately gentle morning saunter along the park's Mace Trail, intent on heeding that outer *and* inner wisdom, latent in what I am seeing *and* what I am feeling. It is still summery warm, for sure, and hardly a leaf is showing a sign of losing its summer green. But the wind is talking, and I am listening. I watch late summer clouds drift across the sky. I notice all these thoughts drifting through me. Autumn is arriving, to the landscape all around me, and to the landscape inside of me. Welcome.

## A Mystery to Solve
*November 2010*

As so often happens after an overnight dusting of snow, my morning walk to the office is distracted by a mystery in the snow. This was the case a couple of days ago. The half inch of new snow was an ideal palette for the pitter patter of animal wanderings captured in their tracks. Halfway down the hill from my house, I noticed a bunch of animal tracks. Five toes, claws registering. At first, I thought racoon, as the commonly seen five-toed track of this general size around here is a bushy-tailed, mask-wearing coon.

But I quickly noticed that these tracks weren't right for a racoon. They were too small, and they were shaped and constructed differently. I've seen so many racoon tracks, as well as fox, and squirrel, and rabbit tracks on my walks to work and around the park. These were different. So, I slowed down and started looking at the details—I had a mystery to solve.

For much of the path of tracks I followed, the front and rear feet appeared to land right in front of the other, almost looking like one long track. In some places, it looked like the rear foot landed right on top of where the front had just been. The long nails of the front foot suggested that this animal likes to dig. The rear track looked a lot like a miniature human footprint. These were not tracks I am used to seeing. Hmm!

When solving a tracking mystery, the actual tracks themselves are only one part of the process. The fact that the tracks were not all that far apart (each set no more than six to eight inches from the previous set) said something of the size of the animal—bigger than a mouse, squirrel or rat, smaller than a coyote. The general direction of travel had a bit of a wandering feel to it. OK, that may be helpful. The five toes were helpful, as canines and felines have four toes, so that eliminated fox or bobcat. I already concluded it wasn't a racoon, and a bear's five-toed tracks would be several times larger. What other critters found around here have five toes? A ringtail does, but their tracks are rounder, and claws are usually not seen or less pronounced in their tracks.

Five toes—OK, I'm getting closer. It must be a member of the weasel family. Otter? No otters around these parts. Badger? Tracks would be much larger. Mink, marten, weasel? Not likely, as I've never seen one in Beulah (although that doesn't mean they may not be here). Wolverine? I wish!

Ah, I've got it. I've been seeing this weasel family member a lot the last several weeks. And smelling it too. I was on the trail of a skunk. And since I've been seeing several skunks with two white stripes down their midnight black bodies, I'd say a striped skunk.

Omnivorous, common in most parts of Colorado (and the whole US), often dormant during cold winter weather (although not a true hibernator), polygamous, about the size of a domestic cat. And, of course, extremely musky, which is its main means of defense.

I've never been sprayed by one, but I helplessly watched my dog Lucy get it right in the face. Tomato juice was ineffective, but a 4:1 mixture of hydrogen peroxide and baking soda, plus a squirt or two of liquid dish soap worked great in getting the smell out. I recall one winter many years ago when several skunks apparently used the crawlspace underneath my bedroom as a den—those were some smelly nights (and the inspiration to properly seal off that crawlspace).

Despite all of this, unless it is very strong, I don't really mind the smell of a skunk. I even kind of like it. I spent most of the first twenty years of my life in New York City, where the air smelled of, well, city things. I guess I associate the musky aroma of a skunk with successfully making the break from the big city and creating a good life for me and my family "in the country," where the smell of a skunk means that one of the neighbors has been by.

## The Last Day of November
*November 30, 2010*

That I've done this a thousand times doesn't make it any less satisfying. Pack on. Out the door. Down the hill. Across the paved road. Into the park. Which trailhead? OK, Tower Trail it is. I pass out of the ponderosas into a sunny south-facing hillside of Gambel oak and mountain mahogany and stop to look around. It's a cool day, but my hat is in my hand as the steady climb and a generous low-in-the-sky sun warm me.

Except for the conifer greens and sky blue, there is little in the way of vivid color on this last day of November. It was a very colorful autumn that seemed to start early and end late. But the deciduous leaves are now all brown, some still clinging to the gray branches, the rest scattered among the dried bunch grasses and late season wildflowers (mostly members of the sunflower family, *Asteraceae*).

A few steps up the trail lead me to the stalk of a Pacific sagewort that still holds a bit of light green in some of its lower leaves. It grew from the ground surrounded by countless pieces of light brown granite with a touch of pink. Several of the rocks host a lichen that is pretty much the same shade of green as the sagewort leaves.

I spy a patch of deep-green moss hiding under a few scraggly oaks. The leaves still attached to the oak branches are small—the biggest no more than three inches long. The lobes are shallow at best; some don't even have lobes. These oaks must be genetically influenced by other *Quercus* species. I've learned that some local Gambel oak (*Quercus gambelii*) have interacted with the pollen from drier-land oak species, drifting on the winds from points south, creating hybrids whose leaves show characteristics unlike the typically deeper lobed Gambel oak leaves.

I notice that a few of the oak leaves are surprisingly not fully brown. One has a red stem and main vein and shows some green and orange. There's a second leaf showing the same colors. And another! OK, there's a bit more color out here than I originally thought. It's subtle, but it's here.

Colorful or not, this land seems to be ready and waiting. The stage is set. Plants have flowered and are now dormant, their life energy stored in their roots and seeds. Migrant birds have headed south, bears are denned up, and the land is ready and waiting—for snow. So am I. By the last day of last November, over forty inches of snow had already fallen. So far this season, barely three inches have fallen, in a handful of dustings. Yesterday's half inch is mostly gone. We are all ready and waiting for snow.

The shadows of a few clouds in the western sky have my hat back on my head and my feet moving. I continue up the trail and get my heart pumping again. I once read that trails not only connect us with each other—before there were roads, foot trails provided the connections between human communities—trails also connect us with ourselves.

Maybe it's some primal memory in a deep recess of my brain, but I feel so at home when walking on a foot trail. Being out here on this trail by myself on this chilly autumn afternoon, even in a snowless and mostly colorless landscape, is exactly where I want to be today. By looking more closely, I discovered that the land, although ready for its winter sleep under a blanket of snow, still has a bit of subtle color. I wonder what else I might discover, about the land, or about myself, on the rest of this trail hike on the last day of November.

**After All These Years, I Finally See One**
*February 2011*

I take one slow, careful step—and I stop. I watch. No reaction. One more step. I stop. I stand as still as I can. Again, the animal doesn't seem to flinch at my presence. My breaths are slow, deliberate, quiet. I can feel my heart beating rapidly in my chest. A few more steps and I am as close as I care to be.

This gorgeous creature, no more than ten feet in front of me, appears totally uninterested in me. What it is interested in are the remains of a lion-killed deer carcass it is devouring, seemingly without pause on my account. Blood from bits of the raw meat still attached to the deer's bones stain a face that is surrounded by ruffs of fur. Underneath the blood stains begin some of the dark streaks that work their way across this ghost feline's lean body.

In over three decades of hiking, backpacking, guiding, teaching and spending countless hours in Colorado's backcountry, I've never seen one of these wild cats. I've seen their scat, I've followed their tracks, I'm certain that they have watched me many times, but, until this hungry and apparently unafraid bobcat showed up in the park a few days ago at a deer carcass we discovered along South Creek, seeing one was unchecked on my list of wildlife sightings. Thanks to this beautiful animal right here in front of me, almost close enough to pet (not that I ever would), bobcat is now checked off!

In my years of teaching students about bobcats, aided by a handsome pelt of mottled browns, grays, black and white, and a skull with large eye sockets and sharp canines, I never realized just how much a bobcat's face looks like a house cat's. The rest of the body, however, is quite different than any house cat I've ever seen. The feline body I am admiring is clearly twice the size of a house cat and it looks extremely powerful—one reason for my cautious and snail-like approach. The black tufts on its erect ears are hard to miss. Although I can't see it right now from this angle, its tail is "bobbed" short, which is why they are called bobcats.

With the speed of cold molasses so I don't startle the cat, I take a few photos. That my presence seems of absolutely no concern to this gorgeous creature reminds me of the aloofness often associated with domestic cats. I suppose that the easy availability of such a plentiful food source the deer carcass is providing, in the middle of winter, is reason enough to tolerate my presence. My experience, at least up until today, is that bobcats are elusive and usually offer only the fleetest of sightings, if any. Needless to say, I am truly appreciating the opportunity to observe this wild cat at such close range.

After nearly an hour, with no sign that the bobcat has any plans to abandon these easy-pickings any time soon, I decide it is time to leave this creature to itself. Offering a silent gesture of thanks for allowing my long intrusion, I slowly back away.

Having witnessed the beauty of one of these mountains' seldom seen residents, I walk home with an even deeper appreciation for this Mountain Park, so full of Nature's wonders.

**It Feels So Good to be Home**
*May 24, 2011*

I take a deep breath. I take another, slowly, deliberately. I want to savor every molecule of delicious air, rich with the fresh scent of the forest released by the rainstorm that rumbled by a short time ago. I haven't been out on this trail for a while, so it feels like I'm coming home after being away for too long.

The forest aromas are only one part of what is beginning to make this hike feel like a splendid little homecoming. The last time I walked this trail it was the tail-end of a dry winter. What were bare oak branches are today covered with new green leaves. The brown winter grasses are greening as well and look vibrantly alive. Maybe it is just because I haven't been here lately, but this fresh color of green is just so pleasing to look at.

The light pink blossoms of spring beauties that were already blooming a couple of months ago are today accompanied by the pink of textile onion; the blues of low penstemon, Nelson larkspur, and Britton skullcap; the orange of western wallflower;

the yellows of mountain bladderpod and golden smoke; and the smiling faces of dwarf daisies, to name a few of the wildflowers I am seeing as I climb the trail. It's as if the land is saying, "Welcome back, Dave, we've missed you."

The happy sounds of birds add to the sense that the forest seems genuinely pleased to see me. A mile or so up the trail, I am now sitting on a favorite rock outcropping with a warming sun on my back, working hard through the clouds to pull the temperature out of the 40s. I glance over my shoulder just in time to see a male western tanager land at the top of a tall Douglas fir, fifty yards away. While hiking, I thought I was hearing the raspy song of this striking red-headed yellow bird that would have recently returned from Central America—seeing it confirms its arrival. The cool moist air seems to have every bird in very good voice, as a second doesn't slip by without the music of birdsong filling it—the music just goes on and on. I am hearing western tanagers, a dusky flycatcher, a broad-tailed hummingbird, yellow-rumped warblers, black-headed grosbeaks… and several I can't readily identify. What glorious music!

Of course, I know it is not the forest, or the wildflowers, or the birds that are happy to see me. The birds would sing just as sweetly, the flowers would bloom just as vibrantly, and the forest would smell just as delicious if I were still stuck in my office immersed in emails, reports, and conversations, or at a meeting somewhere, or doing any of the things that I've let keep me away for so long. I'm only projecting onto the land what I am feeling inside myself. I am the one that has missed the smells and the wildflowers and the birds, and I am the one that is genuinely happy to be out here on this trail, a trail I used to spend so much time on, a trail I know and love so well.

I admit, it's been a struggle for me to find a balance between the countless responsibilities that come with running an organization that works to facilitate a connection between people and Nature, while nurturing my own connection to Nature—particularly to this little pocket of Nature called Pueblo Mountain Park. I have a relationship with this land, and, like any relationship, it requires time and attention to sustain its health. Although much of my time is spent attending to the details of stewarding this land, that is different than nurturing the relationship I have with it. If a parent only provides for a child's physical needs, but spends no time with that child, the relationship will be lacking. The same holds true for the human/Nature relationship—it requires time. And this is what I am recognizing out here right now! It's not the land that is saying "Welcome back," it is me welcoming myself back—to this place that is so special to me.

I am reminded of the words of author and anthropologist Richard Nelson: "Perhaps there are no inherently special places, only places made special by the relationships people sustain with them—wilderness or city, mountain or prairie, desert or swamp, forest or farmland. In this sense, all places on earth are equal and identical, waiting only to be known." Over many years, I have certainly come to know this place, and this knowing has made these trees, these wildflowers and birds and trails—this park—a very special place to me. It feels so good to be back out here right now. It feels so good to be home.

## Why I'm Hiking the Colorado Trail
*July 15, 2011*

As I write these words, I am completely alone at the top of a 12,200-foot ridge separating two drainages that form Mineral Creek in the La Garita Wilderness.

The day's minutes-old sun is warming my back. There isn't a cloud in the sky. To my right is a snow-covered mountain range in the far distance. The wind is calm. The only sound I hear is one bird (maybe a white-crowned sparrow—my alpine bird song identification skills are limited) singing like he is on top of the world. And he is! So am I!

Short, happy-looking alpine sunflowers face the sun, growing from slopes of rock and tundra grasses. Willows, no more than three feet high, add additional texture to this high-altitude landscape. Except for the single bird singing, it is absolutely silent. This sun-warmed morning silence is one of the countless gifts of hiking the Colorado Trail.

I started this backpack along the 486-mile Colorado Trail

more than a year ago, with the intent of hiking it in several shorter outings over two years. The trail exists in 28 segments; I completed Segments 1-15 last year, 268 miles. That left 218 miles through the state's more remote San Juan Mountains for this year. With limited paved-road access and no desire to drive rough jeep roads, I am hiking Segments 16–28 in three separate longer legs this summer. Today is the last day of the first leg, with most of Segments 16-21 through the Cochetopa Hills and La Garita Wilderness behind me.

I'm out here for several reasons. The most public one is to raise revenue for the Nature-education programs of the nonprofit Mountain Park Environmental Center. I'm out here for personal reasons too. You see, I am terminal. Don't be shocked, so are you. We all are. Anyone that is living is going to die. It's that simple. Ever since I hit the half-century mark a few years ago, the stark reality that my body is not going to last forever has given me the push to do some of those things I've always wanted to do, like hike the entire Colorado Trail. It may not be for everybody (apparently not, since I've seen very few others out here), but it's for me.

So here I am, experiencing Nature on its own terms. I've deliberately trimmed the veneer that typically separates most of us from Nature's rawness down to the very bare basics, packed into a modest-sized pack that sits on my back. Being out here with just enough essentials to keep me safe and nourished is a great way to learn about Nature, and about myself.

One thing I've learned is to trust the trail. If I keep putting one foot in front of the other, it will get me there. Another is that how I feel at any given point may very well not be how I feel in an hour. Or in ten minutes. Aches and pains, discouragement, euphoria, loneliness, ease – these all come and go on a long-distance outdoor adventure. Sort of like life itself.

In front of me is a massive, treeless mountain and the trail that will soon take me over several more ridges and, eventually, to Spring Creek Pass. That is where I told Helene I'd meet her, 91 long miles from where I left her at Marshall Pass five days ago. There are still more than ten up-and-down miles to Spring Creek Pass, including Snow Mesa, which, according to the map, is a treeless, relatively flat 12,000-foot-plus plain that would be a dangerous place to be during a thunderstorm. And I know just how quickly these blue skies can turn dark and stormy. But I crawled out of my warm sleeping bag early this morning so I wouldn't have to rush today's miles. I think I'll take a few more minutes to savor this lovely place—and see what else I might learn.

## Flashback on the Colorado Trail
*August 2, 2011*

One slow step follows another. I am hiking up the switch-backs that climb out of the Animas River Valley in the Weminuche Wilderness south of Silverton. At the top of this two-thousand-foot climb is Molas Pass. The pass will mark the end of a fifty-three-mile stretch, the next-to-last leg through Segments 22, 23, and 24 of my Colorado Trail Backpack for Nature Education that brought me through some of the most spectacular scenery I have ever seen.

It's a slow and steady hike through a mixed forest of aspens and conifers. Golden asters, aspen daisies, Indian paintbrush, and goldenrod are some of the wildflowers that are cheering me along the way. I hear the whistle of the Durango and Silverton Railroad locomotive from below, chugging along the tracks I crossed a little while ago. The train would have provided me with an easy way out from the low elevation point of Segment 24 back there, but I am committed to hiking the whole trail, so here I am. I'm not complaining—I am very happy to be right here, making my way up this steep section of the trail.

All of a sudden, I am flashing back to being fifteen years old and trudging up the nine floors of stairs at Brooklyn Tech High School back in New York City. I am at an early morning football workout session, with one of my teammates on my back. Being the smallest and lightest player on the team, I was a popular partner for this grueling activity. Unbeknownst to me then, but I was conditioning for more than football. In fact, my football career lasted only another year, but some of what I would need for all the hiking and backpacking that was ahead in my life was being planted in me on those tough morning stair climbs. I am happy to say that I've never hauled a backpack anywhere near the one-hundred-sixty pounds that I carried on my back forty years ago.

Another train whistle brings me back to the present. I turn around and find a perfect view of the valley far below. A plume of black coal smoke identifies the location of the train that left Durango a couple of hours ago, enroute to the old mining town of Silverton. The train itself, full of tourists and sightseers, looks small and insignificant as it works its way along the river, with the backdrop of the enormous Grenadiers behind it. The Grenadier Range, a sub-range of the San Juan Mountains, is composed of a hard and weather-resistant quartzite. They are striking and majestic and look different than the countless mountains I've seen along the more than four-hundred miles of trail I've hiked so far. Mountains made from this kind of rock are relatively rare in the Southern Rockies. The rounded domes and uniquely shaped peaks remind me of Yosemite.

I turn back and again face the steep trail. I hear the soft call of a western tanager, a colorful bird I have so often enjoyed back in my hometown Mountain Park. The massive trunk of an ancient

Douglas fir catches my eye. When the Weminuche Indians still roamed freely through these mountains, this already a mature tree, growing right here in what is now a federally designated Wilderness area bearing their name. It must have been the remoteness of this steep mountainside that saved it from the logger's saw. For all the nostalgia and romanticism associated with steam locomotives, I prefer the sights and sounds of the forest.

This Colorado Trail Backpack has been many things to me: a physical challenge (and, like many long-term efforts, a mental and psychological challenge), an opportunity to see much of Colorado's beauty, and some additional texture to my busy position as MPEC's Executive Director. It has given me many days of solitude immersed in a variety of Nature's moods, and in my own thoughts. And, thanks to the donations and pledges from so many people, it is providing some very needed support for MPEC's education programs so we can continue to connect young people with the wonders of Nature.

As I continue up the trail, I think back on the thousands of fifth-grade students that have been to MPEC's programs. I know we planted a whole lot of seeds of Nature-connection in those kids, and I hope that maybe some of those seeds will grow big enough to include hiking the Colorado Trail as they get older. But I also know that many of those kids, for various reasons, will likely never hike the Colorado Trail. For them, their hikes in Pueblo Mountain Park as fifth-graders, getting to the Fire Tower and hiking to Devil's Canyon, may very well be the "Colorado Trail Hike" of their lives. All the more reason for me to keep putting one foot in front of the other up this steep mountain—it's for a very good cause!

## Walking Myself Back Home
*September 2011*

*August 25: I am watching storms develop over the ridge just to the west of me. Some look like they have some significant energy in them, but, so far, they all float off to the northeast and miss me. It's around 3pm, and by this time yesterday, it was already raining, and remained chilly, wet and windy until after the sun went down. Most of my trail days through these San Juan Mountains have been wet—time will tell if I get my wish for a rainless day today. So far, so good!*

I wrote those words in my journal from my last night's camp along the Colorado Trail Backpack that has been a big part of my life these last couple of years. I've been off the trail over a week now, and I am still very much in the grasp of this multi-faceted experience. I still feel the deep sense of satisfaction I felt as I hiked that final mile to the trail's terminus in Durango—wow, I walked from Denver to Durango! And I still feel an insatiable appetite for food; after backpacking the last leg of the trek, seventy-four miles over four days with nearly 12,000 feet of cumulative altitude gain, on a diet of low-weight trail food, I am still hungry pretty much all the time.

*From where I am sitting, underneath a scattering of ponderosa pines and a few Douglas firs, I am looking back at the high country where these storms are heading. It looks pretty dark up there.*

"Up there" is where I was that morning—Indian Trail Ridge, part of the last few miles of Segment 27 of the trail's twenty-eight segments. I am so glad I timed that day's hike, my last full day on the Colorado Trail, so I would be across and down from that gorgeously scenic but exposed terrain before the afternoon brought the lightning that accompanied those storms. I am also glad I was not with the couple of fellows I met that morning who told me they were up there the afternoon before, hunkered down and freaked out while the sky was alive with electricity. They said they learned their lesson.

I've been reflecting on what this hike has meant to me. It has certainly been a physical challenge. My rough calculations tell me that I took over one million four hundred sixty-six thousand steps across those 486 miles. I climbed up and back down the equivalent of over three Mt. Everests. With 28 days on the trail, I averaged a bit over 17 miles a day. My longest day was 27 miles, back in Segments 11 and 12 in the Sawatch Range, when I learned that 2000 mountain bikers would soon be racing along that trail section as part of the Leadville 100. That was all the incentive I needed to keep going and get out of their path.

The hike has brought me through six wilderness areas, climbs over numerous passes and high ridges, hot waterless stretches (like the Buffalo Creek burn area), dizzying low-oxygen heights, below freezing nights, cold winds (like on the crest of the Ten-Mile Range above Breckenridge), gorgeous sunrises and sunsets, hikes in the dark (both at the beginning and end of the day), mountain scenery that took my breath away, the color and beauty of countless wildflowers, wild animals and their sign (such as this morning's fresh bear tracks right on the trail). Nature showed me many of her mountain moods, and she showed me much about myself too.

From the journal:

*I hear a Clark's nutcracker, a Steller's jay, the chattering of a pine squirrel in the distance, and now, the wing beats of the nutcracker that was just squawking from the top of one of the ponderosas. There he is—he just landed on the lower dead branch of another ponderosa. Wow, can he squawk loud? There's another nutcracker, and another, and another! I think I'll call this last campsite of mine Clark's Place. I've observed and enjoyed all of these species back home in Beulah and Pueblo Mountain Park.*

*"There's no place like home." I find myself thinking of Dorothy's mantra from the Land of Oz while relaxing in the final camp of this adventure. It's not that I am sorely missing home. It's just that this lovely spot, well, it reminds me of home. After spending the last several hundred miles averaging over 10,000' in altitude, and much of the last 100 miles above treeline, this lower elevation camp feels so much more like where I live and work in Beulah. For the first time since the trail's early miles not far out of Denver, ponderosa pines, which are a familiar and cherished part of my home landscape, are once again a part of my Colorado Trail surroundings. Their orange bark, vanilla aroma, and long needles that, according to John Muir, "give forth the finest music to the wind," are a welcome taste of my home landscape.*

The day after I wrote those words, I continued on the last thirteen miles of the trail. As I dropped further in elevation, it was like I was walking right into Pueblo Mountain Park. The forest became wholly dominated by ponderosas, with a few scattered Douglas firs and an understory of Gambel oak. The spiny leaflets of mahonia, the purple daisies of smooth aster, the *chick-a-dee-dee-dee* of mountain chickadees and the nasal *yank* of red-breasted nuthatches—it's like I walked 486 miles and wound up right back at home. The words of Wendell Berry came to me, "And the world cannot be discovered by a journey of miles, no matter how long, but only by a spiritual journey, a journey of one inch, very arduous and humbling and joyful, by which we arrive at the ground at our feet, and learn to be at home."

I believe that this hike will have meanings to my life well beyond the numbers and physical challenges. For one, it has been a successful fund-raiser for MPEC's education programs. And this idea of walking myself right back home, and Berry's thoughts of learning to be at home at the ground at our feet? These are some of the thoughts I look forward to contemplating over the next weeks and months as I look for the deeper meanings of my Colorado Trail hike.

## I Need to Get Outside
*November 30, 2011*

When it all becomes a little too much—too many tasks, too many conversations, too many have-tos, too many concerns—this is when I know I *need* to get outside and start walking.

It took a little longer than I had hoped, but I finally made it out the door of MPEC. I immediately headed for the part of the park where Nature does pretty much what it wants, the part where I am just a visitor. I needed to be out here, moving my legs, breathing ponderosa air, hearing the wind in the trees and feeling the sun on my face. And so, here I am, doing just that. Like every time before, by the time my feet leave the dirt road and hit the forest floor, all that heaviness already feels lighter.

A hilltop where I haven't been in a long time is calling me. I leave the trail and am working my way through the oak skeletons, bare except for a few straggling brown leaves. The south-facing slope becomes steeper. The gravelly soil has patches of kinnikinnick that I avoid stepping on. Also known as bearberry,

I see none of the red berries that would by now be dried up and brown. The drought made for a bad year for bearberries I reach the top of the hill and am immediately pleased I heard its call. The late November sun is unusually warm, and it seems to have just enough of an edge over the gusty wind. Off comes the pack, out comes the water bottle and journal, and I plop down at the very top of this little knoll.

I sit for a long time and just take it all in. A few dried aster plants still hold the remains of their flower heads, with clusters of tiny seeds waiting for the wind to set them free. Gray stems, with leaves ranging in color from light green to chocolate brown, are covered with countless white hairs. These serve as a wind break, which reduces air flow and decreases rates of transpiration (water loss through evaporation), an important facet of this species' ability to withstand the drought. When it hasn't rained in weeks, and the hot August sun seems relentless, hairy golden asters are often the only flowering plant in these hills. The hairs work.

The steep north side of the hill drops off hard in front of me. I feel the warm sun on my back as I look up into several tall Douglas fir trees. The needled branches, most covered with many brown cones, are dancing in the wind that has settled down into a gentle breeze for a few moments. I examine a cone that has fallen—dried out and seedless, it still has the three-lobed bracts that protrude from between the now-brittle scales, a unique and identifying feature of a Douglas fir cone. The birds are quiet, although the familiar call of a single mountain chickadee lets me know I am not all alone up here. I can hear stronger gusts of wind in the distance, so I will enjoy this relative calm. I know the gusts will soon return to my afternoon journaling place.

The weather report says that this blue sky will soon be turning gray, and the afternoon sunshine will be replaced by a whole lot of snowflakes falling from those gray clouds. The gusty winds that have now found their way back to this spot are trying to tell me, "A storm is on its way." Well, that is just fine with me—this dry hilltop needs all the moisture it can get, and I love being out in the snow just as much as I love being out on this warm and breezy afternoon. Tomorrow, I just may put on some layers and snowshoes and hike right back up here. I am so enjoying this sunshine, but I am just as happy being out in a foot of snow with more flakes falling all around. Just as long as I can break away and get outside.

**Everything is a Miracle**
*March 1, 2012*

If loud and powerful first-day-of-March winds are somehow associated with a large feline, then I guess March has come in like a lion. Last night was one of those ear-plug nights, when a leaping February roared into the month when spring officially arrives, and sleeping was not exactly easy.

I'm not one who often complains about the weather. I can usually swing with whatever is going on outside. The mantra, "There is no such thing as bad weather, only different kinds of good weather," pretty much sums up how I feel most of the time. But I will admit, I've had a touch of the winter blues these last few days. I suppose there is a part of me that is simply ready to ease up on bringing firewood in and keeping the fire going, ready to put my winter jacket in the back of the closet and pull out the shorts and sandals. Don't take this as from someone who dislikes winter. Quite the contrary—I love the snowy landscape (which we've had a nice dose of this winter in Beulah), I love the workout of a hearty cross-country ski or snowshoe, I love bundling up and taking a brisk walk when the temps are in the single digits and the snow is falling. I've enjoyed all of this and more this winter. But truth be told, I am feeling just a little dull? uninspired? gloomy?—I guess I am about ready for winter to move on.

Whether March roars in or not, I find much comfort in knowing that the ancient rhythm of the changing seasons continues on. "There is something infinitely healing in the repeated refrains of nature…the assurance that dawn comes after night, and spring after winter." These words of Rachel Carson capture exactly what I am wanting to take to heart this morning. In fact, it is reaching inside myself and pulling up this very awareness that is one of the antidotes for those occasions when I find myself a little tired of what the season has to offer.

The older I get, the more this fact, that a few degrees tilt of the Earth towards or away from the sun is why there are seasons and all the beauty they bring—spring mornings filled with glorious birdsong, summer rainstorms and rainbows, autumn mountainsides of golden aspen, blankets of winter snow blanketing the land—it just blows my mind.

When I learned this in grade school, it was just another one of those abstract facts that I took at face value so I would get a good grade on the next test. Now that I have a few decades experiencing just what that tilt can do, it seems nothing short of amazing that the Earth keeps revolving around the sun, leaning in and out with each revolution, year after year after year. And from it come gorgeous eight-five-degree summer days filled with wildflower meadows *and* the magic of snowflakes falling from a frozen sky to transform the landscape into a winter wonderland. And from that tilt come a million other wonders of Nature— fearsome windstorms that keep me up at night; gentle autumn days filled with earthy color and pumpkins; majestic summer thunderstorms that can cool down a hot afternoon; four-foot-long icicles hanging off the eaves and glistening in the moonlight; and tiny blue eggs nestled in nests made of twigs and grasses. All of this because our planet tilts a little? Amazing!

Einstein said, "There are only two ways to live your life. One is as though nothing is a miracle. The other is as though everything is a miracle." When I am feeling down about the weather, and the idea that "everything is a miracle" seems very far away from how I am feeling, that is when I need to pull out the awe that comes from realizing what an absolutely beautiful planet I live on. And when I do that, the blues just seem to blow away with the winds, just like the tarp that used to cover my woodpile.

## What Bird Was That?
*May 2012*

A couple of weeks ago, I was walking among the trees with a handful of toddlers and their folks. I always look forward to facilitating Nature Toddlers, MPEC's monthly program for little ones—it gets me out of the office and outside, I get to make some music, and we do some simple Nature exploration activities. I am pretty sure that I get at least as much out of the program as the toddlers do—it is lots of fun for me.

A regular part of the program is introducing a few species of local birds to the little ones, using small bird replicas equipped with authentic song recordings. We had just finished looking for the birds that I had hidden in the brush earlier (the kids just love looking for and finding them) when we heard a real bird up in a nearby tree. It wasn't the song we were hearing—it was a woodpecker hammering away in a small pine tree. The bird seemed oblivious to us and allowed even the littlest ones a good look.

I at first expected to see one of the three more common local woodpeckers—hairy, downy, or flicker—when I noticed a brownish head. Downy and hairy woodpeckers have black and white on their heads (and a red patch on males), and the overall size of this bird was too small for a flicker, which does have some brown on its head. OK, this is a bird I am not so familiar with—I wanted to get a closer and more detailed look. The kids were quickly losing interest, so I did a quick last look—brown head (no red that I could see), brown and white barred back and wings. I was looking for some yellow on its belly, but it was tight up against the tree, so I couldn't see any identifying features of its front.

We rambled on, the bird eventually took off, and it was only a few minutes ago when I remembered that I had seen this bird but hadn't gone any further in figuring out what I had seen (although I had a pretty good idea). I occasionally see a couple of species of sapsuckers in the park—that's why I was looking for the yellow on the front of the body. I was pretty sure this bird was some kind of sapsucker, a type of woodpecker that drills evenly spaced small holes in tree trunks, then returns to feast on the sap and insects that the holes attract.

The field guide gave me the info I needed to make the identification. Both male and female red-naped sapsuckers have red on their heads. I saw no red, so it wasn't a red-naped. Was it a Williamson's? The male Williamson has a black back—my bird did not. OK, it's not the male. The picture of the female Williamson's, which looks quite different than the male, showed the barred back, brown and white, with a brown head, just like I had seen. Success! Had I gotten a look at the front of the bird, I would have seen a yellow belly.

Being an average birder who knows the more common birds in the park and not too many other birds, it is always a pleasure to see a bird I do not know well, and then take the steps to accurately identify it. I am now on the lookout for the male Williamson's, whose bright yellow belly and red throat should be bright and vibrant this time of year with breeding season in the air.

**Hearing the Magic in These Ponderosa Woods**
*May 25, 2012*

The wind in the pines. Crickets. Western wood peewee. Robin. The lovely song of a black-headed grosbeak. Cicadas. Raven. Spotted towhee. Squawks of a Steller's jay. A fly. Mountain chickadee. Grasshopper. It may appear that I am sitting on this slab of light red sandstone all by myself, but my ears tell me I am certainly not alone. On a day that began cloudy and cool with the thermometer barely out of the 30s, the sun-warmed afternoon is alive with the sounds of a ponderosa pine forest in late spring. There are probably some furry creatures nearby, and maybe a few with scales, but most mammals and reptiles around here are usually pretty quiet. It's the birds and the insects that are filling the air with their music.

Much of my wandering hike to this rock today was accompanied by this ponderosa soundtrack. Every landscape has its own soundscape, and these sounds, so familiar and so pleasant to me, are a cherished part of my home landscape. If I were sitting on a rock four miles east of where I am now, the sounds would not be the same. I'd be in a landscape with many more pinyons and junipers, and the calls of pinyon jays, of which there are none here right now, would be prevalent. Another few miles east, and there would be the sounds of the shortgrass prairie—the iconic song of western meadowlarks, the shrill call of an American kestrel, probably more grasshoppers. Few of the sounds surrounding me now would be out there.

As I bring my attention back to my sitting spot among the ponderosas, I hear the less musical song of a western tanager. Western tanager, black-headed grosbeak, American robin—these three birds have similar sounding songs that are sometimes confused with one another. This is how I learned to tell them apart—the grosbeak sounds like a robin who took singing lessons, while the tanager sounds like a robin with a sore throat. All three of them are singing within earshot right now.

There's another familiar sound, the nasal call of a white-breasted nuthatch. And another, the unmistakable racket of a northern flicker's song. It's a wild symphony orchestra out here, and I am sitting right smack in the middle of it.

This reminds me of the one time I got to perform with a symphony orchestra. Prior to opening MPEC, I made a living as a musician. Almost all of the million performances I did (at least, that's how many it seems like I did) were part of a duo with my wife, Helene. Our two vocals and my one guitar were it, and I loved the simple sparseness of two-part harmony and whatever I could get out of those six strings.

Once, early in my career, I got a call from the conductor of the Pueblo Symphony. The classical guitarist scheduled to do a guest performance on a Spanish piece had to cancel due to an accident, and they needed a sub—tomorrow. I met with the conductor, we ran through the piece with only his piano and my guitar, and I rehearsed it on my own several times. The next evening, there I was on stage in a borrowed tux, surrounded by a symphony orchestra with all of those instruments—violins, clarinets, trumpets, cellos, flutes, violas, oboes. It was wonderfully grand, hearing the modest sound of my guitar and the diverse array of sounds being made with these instruments, combining to make such glorious music.

That evening performance truly was a magical moment in my career. Yet, I can't help but feel that there is just as much magic right here in these ponderosa woods, surrounded by all this natural music. Instead of being one of the music makers, today I am in the audience, and I'm loving the performance. It is a different kind of harmony, a rather chaotic rhythm and tempo, but this symphony of Nature's sounds is such welcome music to my ears.

## We are All Waiting for Rain
*September 3, 2012*

It's rather quiet in the park this evening. I do notice the *yank-yank* calls of several red-breasted nuthatches and a few crickets as I settle into an off-the-trail sitting spot to take it all in. As I adjust to the stillness of this place after walking hard uphill to get here, I realize it is not as quiet as I originally thought. The lack of human-made sounds is what made it initially seem quiet, but there's quite a bit going on around me in the non-human world. A Steller's jay and a mountain chickadee make their presence known, and now the percussive sounds of a few raindrops hitting the oak leaves join in.

No sooner that I feel the wetness of a few drops on my arms does a little breeze kick up, and the raindrops disappear.

"Everything has a story." I read a book review yesterday, and while the book's title escapes me, what stuck with me is this statement about stories quoted from the book. I look up and see countless stories surrounding me. I see a flicker at the top of a brown-needled white fir tree. The tree is dead. The bird soon flies off and disappears into the evening. The leaves on the stand of oaks near where I am sitting are all brown and dried-out, as if it were November. I don't believe the oaks are dead, but they apparently gave up their wait for rain, skipped any semblance of autumn color, and went right into late fall mode—and we're only a few days into September.

The breeze has become a stronger wind as a Steller's jay squawks away nearby. I can't say for sure, but if I could somehow understand the meaning behind these squawks, it would not surprise me if they meant something like, "Come on, rain already!"

I look around me at some other oaks still holding on to some green in their leaves, and a stand of Douglas firs, and a scrawny young Rocky Mountain juniper, and small clumps of grass that are more brown than green. All these species and I are right here in this spot, feeling the wind coming out of a gray southwestern sky. Despite the differences between us, I suspect there is at least one common thread in our stories—we are all waiting for rain.

As I write these words in my journal, the wind gets even stronger. But for an occasional stray raindrop, it's another dry storm with plenty of wind—and no rain!

If I were to write the story of the summer of 2012, a good title for it could be "Waiting for Rain." Just yesterday, what appeared to be a nice rainstorm brewing in the sky left only three hundredths of inch of water in the rain gauge.

As much as I wish it wasn't so, and it's certainly not the first time, but I believe the drought is getting to me. I am trying to stay above it! There are still a few wildflowers in bloom—Kansas gayfeather, several species of asters, and goldenrod—so it could be even drier. The extremely dry summer of 2002 saw essentially no blooming wildflowers in the park, save for one species of aster. I've been trying to take to heart a line from a David Wilcox song, *All the roots grow deeper when it's dry.*

So, yes, I'm trying to stay positive, and I know it could be so much worse. Even so, I still find myself in the "waiting for rain" mindset. Now that it is September, with the colder months just ahead, it will soon change to "waiting for snow."

**Immersing Myself in Nature**
*December 2, 2012*

"It is harder to get caught up in the natural mysteries of the planet than it used to be." I am not sure if this rings true for true for everyone, but my hunch is it does. It certainly does for me. I clipped out the article that contained these words from a magazine over a year ago and pasted it into my journal.

I like to read the article now and then because it reminds me that I must continue to pry myself away from the endless distractions and get myself outside as often as I can. I may run a Nature education center and a Mountain Park, but my position keeps me in the office way more than I care to admit. Sure, I do get out in the park as a part of my job, but when I am out, it's often an eroded trail, or a rough section of road, or a part of forest we are mitigating for wildfire that is my focus. I am aware of the Nature around me when I am addressing these issues—the warmth of the sun, the bite of the wind, what wildflowers are in bloom where I am—but it is different than being out with the deliberate intent of immersing myself in the natural world.

So, here I am, tucked away among the shrubby vegetation on a familiar hillside after a fast-paced, sweat-producing hike up the Northridge Trail. The impacts of the drought are hard to ignore—the lack of snow (it is December 2, after all, and not a patch of white can I see around me, near or far), the brown-needled conifers that recently succumbed to the lack of moisture, the dusty trail. My mind is again tempted into bemoaning the dryness, as well as the climate changes caused by our species' activities that are likely exacerbating the dry stretches of weather that are a natural part of this landscape—not to mention the weather patterns everywhere that are being turned upside down. But not today!

I look around me and notice the yellow stalks on numerous yuccas; they were covered in large creamy white flowers not all that long ago during a wetter spring season. Down the hill in front of me are several Douglas firs loaded with cones, also a product of adequate spring moisture. A few red-breasted nuthatches are sounding their duck-like squawk of a call.

All around me are clumps of grasses, many with a prolific crop of seeds at the top of their stems; I even see a few blades of green at their bases. A rock the size of two lop-sided basketballs is right beside me, a chunk of red granite covered with pale green lichens with wavy appendages. I look closer and see at least three other species of lichens—a black one, a gray one, and a bright yellow one. The scrawny mountain mahogany bush just down the hill from the rock still holds a few brown leaves. A closer look reveals what appear to be many tiny hairs covering the leaves—it looks like peach fuzz. The plant's new stems are also covered with these tiny hairs, a moisture-preserving adaptation common in plants that grow in arid environments. The music of several pygmy nuthatches, high-pitched and oh-so-busy, is coming from a tall ponderosa pine a hundred feet to my left.

The article pasted in my journal says that "immersion in a place, or in a moment, can transform your relationship with the wild." How true. In the short time I've been sitting here, the drought, under this blue-sky sunshine that is beginning to feel downright hot, remains. But my quiet observations of a few of the members of this hillside community in this Mountain Park have welled up inside of me a strong feeling of gratitude for having this place—this park—to immerse myself in, to care for, to find peace in.

## An Old Tree, An Old Friend
*February 21, 2013*

There is a snag that has stood watch on this hilltop for as long as I can remember. It isn't very tall, maybe thirty feet. Its bark was long ago lost to the elements; it stands gray and weathered with gnarly branches. This snag and I go way back, like an old friend that is always there, always on this hilltop. It is just west of an orange granite outcrop, a favorite sitting spot of mine, not far from where the Mace Trail meets the Tower Trail.

I remember a time, it must be twenty years ago now, when I would visit that granite every few days for several weeks, contemplating a difficult family situation I was dealing with. The tree was already a snag then, and it just stood, tall and strong, as I wrote pages and pages in my journal. This old tree was also right there with me when I'd sit near its base and think and write and scheme and plan for what would eventually become the Mountain Park Environmental Center.

There was the time I heard the call of a bird I did not

recognize. It eventually landed on one of the snag's twisted branches and stayed long enough for me to identify my first Clark's nutcracker. I remember hiking up here one summer morning when it was still dark to watch the sun rise. On so many loop hikes that I've guided that climb up the Mace Trail and then down the Tower Trail, I would point to the snag up ahead to a group of out-of-breath hikers. "Once we reach that point," I'd say, "it's all downhill the rest of the way."

This spot is one of my usual locations for the "music" part of many Full Moon Music Hikes I've guided over the years. Hundreds and hundreds of hikers have sat on this hillside (not all at once—I did say *many* hikes, not just one), listening to me and my guitar while watching the moon rise out of the saddle on the ridge to the east. If you put your ear right up against the snag's trunk, you just might hear a few lines of Sweet Baby James, a song I've sung here many times. *Deep greens and blues are the colors I choose / Won't you let me go down in my dreams?*

I hiked up here a few weeks ago and discovered that the snag is no longer standing sentinel over this special place. It has withstood years and years of wild winds that usually come roaring out of the southwest, sometimes with hurricane force. Well, sometime not that long ago, a powerful gust finally ended the snag's reign of standing watch over this part of the park. As I write this little essay, I am sitting not under but *on* the base of the snag's weary trunk. When it fell, it landed on a small but stout pinyon pine. So, it is not sitting directly on the ground, but leaning at around a twenty-degree angle from the land. It is pointing towards the northeast—evidence that it was one of those fierce southwest winds that brought it down.

No, it is no longer standing tall like it has for many decades—both as a live tree and then as a standing dead tree. But there is no need for me to say good-bye to this old tree friend of mine, as it will still be hanging around this hilltop for many more decades. I am sure that, regardless of how many more years I have left, there will still be the remains of this old tree right here where it fell, with the same pretty view of the wild lands to the west that I am looking at right now, long after I take my last hike. And then, many more years after that, there will be a new tree growing from this same hilltop. It will be nurtured by this snag as its decomposed remains become a part of the soil and are absorbed by and become a part of that new tree. And many years after that, the new tree will die, eventually fall, and the process will keep cycling, over and over again, just as it has for a long, long time.

### Reflections of a Grandfather
*May 27, 2013*

It is flying away from the pond, then banks hard to its right and drops thirty feet in two seconds. Flying just above the pond's surface, it skims the water for the briefest moment, then rises to the level of the treetops in just two seconds. All of that for what had to be a very small drink of water. It repeats this several times and is soon joined by several others. The swallow—a violet-green swallow that has returned to the park for the summer—didn't seem to mind the strange watercraft drifting lazily across the middle of the pond. I am here on this summer-like day in late May with my 9-year-old grandson, Jude, and his friend Brian. Well, I *was* here with them—they just took off on their bikes and left me at the pond to monitor their somewhat pond-worthy creation.

As they were finishing their breakfast of home-made waffles and fresh fruit earlier this morning, after a night of "camping" in the playhouse I built for Jude and his little sister Scarlett on my little chunk of forest just across from the park, Jude proclaimed, "Let's build something!" They decided on building a boat. I steered them away from a boat big enough to hold the two of them ("We don't have the time or the materials for that large of a project."), so off they went to my stash of lumber to find the makings for a somewhat smaller watercraft. I soon followed and was instructed to cut some boards to the length they needed. I coached them as they nailed them together in the design they came up with. I gave them a few hints on how to construct a sail, and off they went, looking for just the right diameter stick for a mast. Before long, their yellow-sailed work of art was ready for its maiden voyage.

"Try it here where the water is shallow, in case it doesn't float," I suggest. "Good idea!" is their response. They release it and watch it list heavily to one side, but it does not sink. A breeze grabs the sail and off it goes across the pond. Happy that it didn't sink, they are already scheming on how to improve the design. "If we put a board across the back" Jude ponders, "do you think it wouldn't tilt so much?" While the boat makes its way to the pond's far shore, we talk about some modifications we could make later. The swallows continue swooping all around. The boys run to the other side of the pond and send it out again. After a few minutes, they decide to leave me at the pond and take off on their bikes to other parts of the park. Few things could make me happier than knowing that these two boys are getting to play, explore, ride their bikes, and be in Nature today.

I watch the swallows, hear the song of a mountain chickadee, notice how a gust of wind really gets the boat moving, and reflect on the countless children that have played, explored, wondered, and learned on the shores of this little pond. Tomorrow, when Jude and Brian are back in their third-grade classrooms, another fifty or sixty or seventy 5th-graders will be in the park, exploring, playing, and learning in Nature's magical "outdoor classroom," right here in Pueblo Mountain Park. And how, in a few weeks, groups of MPEC summer campers will be trekking all over the park. Sometimes I think that there is a blurry similarity between how my days *off* work and how my days *at* work look. No, I am not out with kids as much as I used to be, but my work at MPEC is still very much about bringing children to Nature. Whether it is my grandson and his buddy, or the thousands of children that have participated in MPEC programs (and the thousands that will participate in the future), I believe that there are few things I will ever do in my life that are more important than creating opportunities for kids to be outside.

The swallows continue their acrobatics as the boys make their way back to the pond. "How's the boat?" "It's doing good," I say, and then suggest, "Hey, check out that bird flying above the pond." They follow it with their eyes as it zigs and zags and then skims across the water, leaving the tiniest of wakes as it rises off the water and into the treetops. "Cool!" they both say in unison.

**Taking Stock of My One Precious Life**
*July 2013*

Forty-two degrees—rather cool for mid-July. I step outside for some warm morning sun and instantly notice the neon blue of a male western bluebird, perched on the roof. It drops to the brick patio, finds an insect, and makes a beeline to the nest box hanging on a small pine twenty feet from the north side of my house. I hear the nestlings clamoring for some morning nourishment.

I slowly walk the fifty feet to the top of where my property slopes down into the woods. I can hear water crashing through the creek bed down below. Three days ago, it was drought dry. Four plus inches of rain that deluged the land in less than twenty-four hours has the creek alive once again. I'm not here thirty seconds, scanning the woods while savoring the sound of the creek, when a bear lumbers out of the trees off to my right, two hundred feet down the hill. It is heading straight for me. I decide to stay perfectly still and see what it does.

It is a healthy looking, completely black, black bear.

Whoever named *Ursus americanus* the black bear apparently didn't bother to notice that more than half of this species in Colorado is some shade of brown, some as light as cinnamon. But this black bear is quintessentially black. Judging by its size, I'd say it is about three years old, maybe four—not huge, but not small either.

I've made every effort to make my property unattractive to bears, which, in essence, means that I've eliminated any easy meals. Once I knew that my beary neighbors had awakened from their long winter's sleep, I quit feeding the birds, I no longer put kitchen scraps in the compost pile, and trash only goes out just before the weekly trash truck arrives. So, there is no good reason for this bear to be messing around my house—it must just be passing through. It does not appear to be in any kind of hurry, but it is getting closer. If the bear is aware of me, it makes no indication of it. I notice a slight breeze is moving across the hill from the direction of the bear, so its keen sense of smell wouldn't have picked me up yet. Just as that thought crosses my mind, the bear veers to its right and heads towards my neighbor's place down the hill. A closer encounter of the *Ursus* kind does not appear to be on this day's list of adventures.

Just as the bear changes direction, a doe and its spotted fawn bolt out of the brush and in seconds are out of the scene. They must have been bedded down and took off as soon as they became aware of the bear, which, as far as I can tell, paid them no mind as it continues on its unhurried saunter across the lower part of my woods.

The bear soon melts into the Gambel oak and is gone. I am now the lone mammal on the hillside. A violet-green swallow sails by me and enters another nest box to my left. I hung that box on a large ponderosa pine tree twenty years ago and noticed this spring that it is leaning and needs another nail. But the swallows moved in before I could get to it, so I guess a crooked nest box is not a problem for violet-green swallows.

I see movement on the forest floor ten yards in front of me. A least chipmunk—named for its diminutive size—darts up to and over a pile of firewood stacked in the woods. I guess my tenure as the hillside's only mammal is up. Unlike the bear, which moved with a steady grace, this little critter can't seem to make up its mind where it wants to go. It slips between a couple of logs, shoots across the ground to another pile of wood, darts out and appears to smell a clump of grass, then disappears in another wood stack. Wow, can that little rodent move quickly! All the while, the bluebird continues bringing food to its offspring—there it goes with a large-winged insect in its beak.

It's been merely five minutes since I stepped out the door. To think, I've witnessed all of these natural happenings, unfolding just outside the walls of my house, in only five minutes. How much more would I see, I wonder, if I stayed right here for an hour, or all morning, or all day? I once read that Henry David Thoreau sat in one place for an entire day watching a spider on its web. His Concord neighbors thought he was a lazy oddball, wasting his time watching a spider, or aimlessly sauntering over the countryside, or living in a tiny cabin next to some remote pond. Henry David had some of his own thoughts about those neighbors:

> …sometimes I am reminded that the mechanics and shopkeepers stay in their shops not only all the forenoon, but all the afternoon too, sitting with crossed legs, so many of them, - as if the legs were made to sit upon, and not to stand or walk upon, - I think that they deserve some credit for not having all committed suicide long ago.

The thing is, unlike most summer mornings of the past nearly four decades (as well as mornings of every other season), when I'd be "off to the races" chasing my music career, or more recently, creating and running a not-for-profit Nature education center, today I could, if I chose to, sit here all day and watch these woods. And I could tomorrow too, and the next day, and next week, and next month too, if I wanted to. No, I am not unemployed, and I am not sick, and I am not retired. I am simply taking a break.

Somehow, the calendar on my office wall says July 2013. This doesn't really make sense to me, because just a year or two ago, or so it seems, the calendar read July 1976. Somehow, in what seems like just a handful of years, I went from being a just-married, barely out of my teens, head-full-of-dreams young man newly landed in these southern Colorado foothills to a fellow realizing that the age of sixty is just over the near horizon. Me, almost sixty? How in the world did I get here?

The truth is, all these years have been full and rich and ever so busy molding many of those dreams into reality. It's been a great ride, it truly has. But while I worked and schemed and worked so much more in making all those dreams come true, I somehow failed to notice just how fast the world was spinning.

So, here I am, a couple of weeks into a two-month leave that I managed to craft for myself from my Executive Director position. I am moving slowly on this perfect morning, noticing the details of this wooded hillside and all that has happened in it in just five minutes. For these precious summer days in this one precious life of mine that is flying by, after so many years filled with working to try to make the world a little bit better, I am free to occupy my mind and my body and my days with bears, and birds, and spiders, and Thoreau, and aimless saunters. And my family, and my love of books, and music, and writing, and where my life has been, and where my life is going.

When this break is over, I have every intention of continuing to share my humble contributions to making my community, and this world, a better place. But, after only a couple of weeks, I am noticing that this break is already changing my perspective on things like work, and livelihood, and balance, and how fast life seems to be going by, and what I want my next four decades (or two decades, or three years, or as little or as much time as I have left) to be filled with. I have a feeling that, when these few weeks are up and this break is over, I will be spending many more mornings standing on this hilltop, watching these woods, looking for bear and deer and foxes and bluebirds, noticing the leaves on the oaks changing color this fall… And, as soon as the swallows have moved out of that crooked nest box, I am going to climb up there and fix it.

## Seasons of Change
*August 28, 2013*

A soft breeze moves across the moisture on the back of my t-shirt, sweaty from being underneath the small backpack that I just took off. My back feels cool while the rest of me is quite toasty. A late summer heat wave is in full swing, and the morning sun only makes the air seem hotter. It certainly feels like summer on this hilltop where I just sat down. Yet, despite all this heat, I can sense that a change is in the works. I can see it in the angle of the sun and the texture of the sunlight, as if the light itself speaks in light waves that summer is winding down.

I can see the change on the land. Where a few weeks ago there were penstemons and wallflowers all along the trail, this morning the trail was graced with so many late season wildflowers—sunspots, four o'clocks, many species of asters— all in happy bloom. The soundscape was alive in bird song and was inescapable to my ears when I sat on this hilltop earlier in the summer. It is not without the sounds of birds this morning—

I listen carefully and hear a flicker, a chickadee, a robin, a Steller's jay, a towhee. But the bird music this morning sounds more like a sparse avant-garde piece with generous use of rests between somewhat sporadic bird calls. This is quite the change from the full-on symphony of bird song that was blasting around this place a couple of months ago.

When I return here in a few weeks, most of those happy blossoms will have become brown, dried out flower heads, the oak leaves will no longer be green, the sun will be weaker and lower in the sky, and the breeze will be chillier. A few weeks further, and the oaks will be leafless, the grasses will all be brown, maybe poking up through a layer of white, and I will have traded this t-shirt and pair of shorts for several layers of insulation from the air that will be many degrees colder than it is right now.

The only thing constant in life, as they say, is change. This truth is never more apparent than to those who take the time to pay attention to what is happening in the natural world around them. Being a part of Nature, and in spite of our efforts to sometimes prevent it, change is a constant with people, and with all of our activities and enterprises too. Birth, aging, injury, education, marriage, sickness, death, construction, destruction, economic booms, economic struggles, new jobs, lost jobs, new businesses, failing businesses... Everything in our lives and families and workplaces and the circles in which we live is moving, evolving, growing, shrinking, starting over, ending, morphing into something that maybe we expected, but probably just as often, we never expected. Everything is changing.

I pause in my writing and notice that all the birds are quiet. A full minute passes before I hear the call of a chickadee, way off in the woods. Even in the course of an hour, change is constantly underway.

I look around and see brown-needled trees peppering the

green hillsides. I take notice of the young ponderosa pine in whose shade I am sitting. If insects or drought or fire do not get to it, maybe it will become a massive two-hundred-year-old tree someday. Or maybe not. One thing is for sure, though, this tree will not stay just as it is—it will grow, or weaken from disease, or blow over in a windstorm. It will change!

As I look out at this very familiar yet ever-changing mountain landscape that surrounds me, these poetic biblical words of wisdom that Peter Seeger adapted and set to his lovely melody find their way to this hilltop: *To everything turn, turn, turn / there is a season turn, turn, turn / and a time to every purpose under heaven.*

## Winter has Arrived—Welcome
*November 25, 2013*

A lone snowflake drifts out of a slate-colored sky and finds its way onto the page of my journal that I am writing on. A woodpecker squawks.

I trudged through over a foot of new snow to get to this somewhat protected place along a path I have walked a thousand times. In precipitation of every variety, in sunlight, in moonlight, in violent winds that brought down trees, in every condition have I walked that path. Today, I walked it as it wound its way through a world magically transformed. Yesterday it was a late fall landscape of browns and grays. Today the land is covered in a fresh blanket of pure white.

A small band of juncos flits by and disappears into the branches of a Rocky Mountain juniper. I can no longer see those busy little gray birds, but the dense evergreen foliage, dappled white with snow, is alive with their many tiny calls, squeaks, and clicks.

The storm's prolific snowfall was a surprise to wake up to this morning. After nearly an hour of shoveling the snow from the various walkways around my property, its heavy wetness is now well imprinted on my tired arms, shoulders and back. The sky appeared to be in the early stages of clearing out while I was shoveling earlier today, but the little bit of blue sky was soon covered again with ominous looking snow clouds.

After a night of heavy snow, it's been snowing lightly since this morning's first light, but that one snowflake that landed on this page a little while ago was one of the storm's last. The snow clouds now appear to be breaking up for real. The western sky is beginning to be dressed in fair weather clouds, backlit by the late afternoon sun. The temperature, which hovered in the mid-thirties all day, feels like it is dropping. I'm beginning to cool down—I'll be moving along soon.

A chickadee calls from a ponderosa pine, its branches covered in what look like overly generous dollops of whipped cream. This landscape is a picture postcard of peace and beauty. Except for the birds, I hear nothing else. I stop writing and take it all in. I eventually hear the sound of a crow, coming from above. I look up and see dozens of crows, widely spaced and flying out of the north. I can tell they are crows and not ravens by the continuous flapping of their wings. Unless it is very windy, ravens usually flap once or twice, then soar. I see that the backdrop of sky has a larger percentage of blue than it did just a little while ago. The sun has slipped behind the western ridge, and the clouds have turned a peachy yellow.

I am moved by the sublime perfection of this moment. I pause and realize it is more than a moment. The whole time that I've been sitting here, writing, experiencing the winding down of the storm, watching a fair-weather sky move in behind the storm, has been nothing short of magic. Just as the sky has morphed from looking gray and mean into a gentle peaceful sky, I too feel completely different than when I sat down here a short hour ago. Not that I was pre-occupied, or keyed up, or feeling burdened when I first arrived, but being here has filled me with a deep calmness that I cannot help but notice. Magic!

I also notice that the dropping temperature has me feeling downright cold. Time to move on. I put on my pack and notice that the clouds are now pink. A crisp, cold evening is well underway, and I cannot think of another place I would rather be. As I head down the path, I say out loud into the cold evening air, "Winter has arrived. Welcome!"

## Why I Go to Nature
*September 4, 2014*

*That's why I'm here / That's why I'm here.* This simple refrain from a James Taylor song is accompanying me as I leave the road and lazily work my way along the trail to Devil's Canyon. It may be September, the month when autumn officially begins, but it is still a hot summer day today, with triple digits mentioned on the radio this morning for parts of Colorado. I am not up for all that sun, so I am opting for the park's shadiest trail.

That's why I'm here now, sitting on the cool floor of the park's iconic canyon. Well, the cool shade is one reason I'm here in this part of the park. Of course, I could have just stayed indoors to avoid the heat of the sun. There is a lot more to why I am here among these towering granite walls than to find a spot of shade. Why do I routinely go out into wild Nature? As I ponder this question, I look up and see a cloudless bluer-than-blue sky framed by the pink, gray and green walls of the canyon. One wall is in bright sunshine, the other—the one I am sitting at the base of—is all shade.

The near canyon wall just to my right is covered in a sizable patch of rich green moss, interspersed with lichens of several colors—pea soup green, creamy gray, fluorescent yellow/ green, dull gray… The rock itself may not be alive, but there is life all over it. Here and there are some tenacious plants that have found just enough of a crack to grow in—a small golden aster about to open a couple of yellow flower heads; a few grasses boasting healthy heads of seed; the blossoms of a couple of goldenrod; and a handful of flowerless small shrubs—waxflower and mountain ninebark.

I narrow my focus to a few square inches and find a short white hair clinging to the branch-like appendages of a moss; a tiny red spider mite; the cell-like structures of a light gray lichen; another hair, much longer and brown (probably unknowingly left here by a hiker who rested in this same spot); the dried out wings of a small butterfly; a strange looking ant, maybe a millimeter long, that seems to float over and not walk on the rock.

A strong gust of warm wind forces its way down through the narrow canyon and takes my focus away from the rock. I listen to the many sounds associated with it—the subtle rustling of the needles on some nearby white firs; an oak leaf moving across the rocks strewn over the canyon floor; the bigger sound of the wind whipping through the crowns of the trees further down the canyon. I hear the call of a canyon wren and hope that it will break into its iconic canyon song.

Seeing, feeling and hearing all of this is the main reason why I am here. I go to Nature to break free, at least for a little while, from the weight of days full of too many things to think about and too many things to do, to get away from the mental clutter that so often accompanies living in our fast-paced, modern world. Nature is my doctor's office, my therapist's couch, my sanctuary and church. Nature is my meditation, and it is my medication. Nature is my real home, and the lichens and the birds and the wind are my friends.

The wind has settled down and the canyon has become a much quieter place. I keep listening for the magical song of the canyon wren, but not yet. A chattery squirrel breaks the silence, soon followed by the scratchy squawk of a Steller's jay.

## Fifty Years of Wilderness
*September 2014*

It was a sunny summer day in 1964, I was an eight-year-old New York City boy, and my grandparents took me to the New York State World's Fair in Flushing Meadow Park. The Fair's corporate exhibits by the likes of General Motors, General Electric, Ford, Walt Disney, and RCA were introducing my spongy brain to some of the technological wizardry that they envisioned would become the world that I would grow up to live in. I don't remember that many details, but I remember the tall steel model of the Earth that became one of the icons of the Fair, and remains to this day in Flushing Meadow Park.

Beyond the optimism of the World's Fair, 1964 was an eventful year—the Beatles came to America, race riots were blowing up in many U.S. cities, and our nation's involvement in the Viet Nam War was accelerating. Most of these events never made it into my 8-year-old consciousness (although my family happened to be driving by JFK airport on the evening that the

Beatles first landed in the States, so I was aware them). Another significant event of that year, which I only learned about several years later, was the signing on September 3 of the Wilderness Act by President Johnson.

Here we now are in 2014, and many folks are acknowledging and celebrating the 50th Anniversary of the signing of the Wilderness Act. I am one of them. I didn't know it then, but I have since developed a deep sense of pride that our nation has adopted the Wilderness Act. Here is some language from the Act and where that pride stems from:

> In order to assure that an increasing population, accompanied by expanding settlement and growing mechanization, does not occupy and modify all areas within the United States and its possessions, leaving no lands designated for preservation and protection in their natural condition, it is hereby declared to be the policy of the Congress to secure for the American people of present and future generations the benefits of an enduring resource of wilderness.
>
> A wilderness, in contrast with those areas where man and his own works dominate the landscape, is hereby recognized as an area where the earth and its community of life are untrammeled by man, where man himself is a visitor who does not remain.

For most of our existence, the human species existed in wilderness. That is no longer the case. Most of our lives are now dominated by the fruits and trappings of our modern technological world. Not all of what I saw at the 1964 World's Fair has come true, but the overall vision of a high-tech society was spot on—we now live in a society built around technology.

The year 1964 may have expressed a vision of a world of amazing technologies, but paradoxically, the year also produced the Wilderness Act. This forward-thinking piece of legislation expresses the other side of the coin by preserving and protecting Wilderness Areas that are an antidote to the frenzied pace that is so much a part of our technological lives. Wilderness is a refuge—not only for escaping the weight of civilization and technology, but also a refuge for wildlife, for clean air and water, and for the human spirit. Wilderness Areas are where we can re-create that ancient bond that we have with wild places. In a sense, going to wilderness is going home.

To me, the Wilderness Act also represents a turning point in our nation's history. The Wilderness Act exhibits a measure of humility, a desire to actually put a limit on ourselves, to say that these places are to be left alone. I feel a deep sense of gratitude for the people that worked so hard to bring the Wilderness Act into existence—Howard Zahniser, Arthur Carhart, Bob Marshall, Aldo Leopold, and Olaus and Mardy Murie. The name Arthur Carhart should be familiar to those who are familiar with MPEC. Carhart, who was the visionary behind Pueblo Mountain Park, and whose vision MPEC is carrying into the 21st century, is often referred to as "the chief cook in the kitchen during the critical first years" of the wilderness movement.

Carhart was a lifelong wilderness advocate, yet he ultimately chose to oppose the Wilderness Act, as he was heartsick with its compromises and felt it needed to provide stronger protections for wilderness. But his place in the development and eventual signing of the Wilderness Act into law cannot be overstated. That MPEC, an organization which exists to provide a place where we can step out of our frenzied lives and re-connect with ourselves and the natural world, operates in a park that was created by such a wilderness advocate is, at least to me, no mere coincidence.

\* \* \*

Postscript
*February 2023*

In the years that have elapsed since I wrote this essay, my understanding of the concept of Wilderness has evolved—enough so that I feel it important to briefly share some of my thinking on this topic.

Something that I was aware of, but, admittedly rather peripherally when this essay was written, is the fact that many of these wild lands were never, as the Wilderness Act says, "untrammeled by man, where man himself is a visitor who does not remain." This view of wild places as being untouched by humans is a myth. Our country's Native Americans have been occupying, influencing and shaping these lands for thousands of years prior to colonization by Europeans. They diverted water for irrigation, they used fire to improve wildlife habitat, they constructed farms, and they built communities. They were very much a presence, even in places that are now Wilderness Areas.

That being said, I feel that there is a huge difference between the ways Native Americans occupied, used and viewed lands and waters, and the ways modern Americans occupy, use and view lands and waters. Unlike Indigenous peoples' relatively gentle footprint on the natural environment, our country's impact on Nature is driven by an economic system that requires continual quantitative growth, aided by ever-more-advanced technologies—and have a huge destructive footprint.

Native peoples never differentiated between "wilderness" and "non-wilderness"—they saw no reason to "protect" certain areas from themselves. Their use of land did not, and could not, subject Nature to the level of destructiveness, poisoning, over-use, disregard, degradation, and disrespect that our modern civilization is capable, and guilty of.

Hence, it still makes complete sense to me that, unlike in Native Americans societies, lands and waters—and all of Nature—in these modern United States need protection. We need some places—as many places as possible—that are free, to the degree that is possible, from the destructive impacts of our fast-paced, high-tech, modern ways of living. I continue to be a whole-hearted supporter of our system of federally protected Wilderness Areas.

**Emphatically Silent**
*December 2, 2014*

Lookout Point. I don't know why, but when I set aside the afternoon of this day to be out in the park, Lookout Point kept coming up as where I needed to be. So, here I am, on this lichen covered hunk of granite that looks out over Devil's Canyon, and the countless trees climbing the ridge to the southwest, and the meadows that surround the old rodeo arena. Attached to the rock is a pipe railing, dark brown with age. A small patch of cement has the date Oct. 17, 1934 carved into it, indicating a date when this railing was worked on up here.

All alone on this ancient rock under a gentle sky, I can't help but notice just how quiet this place is. I pause to listen, and I hear no sounds at all for long stretches. Except for the very occasional call of a mountain chickadee, a Steller's jay, and a Townsend's solitaire, Lookout Point is bathed in complete silence—and so am I!

The sound of my pen moving across the page of my journal

is even an intrusion, so I stop writing. Minutes go by. The silence continues. The weak sun becomes a bit stronger as a thin cloud slips past it. More silence. Thoreau wrote in his journal that "The longest silence is the most pertinent question most pertinently put. Emphatically silent. The most important questions, whose answers concern us more than any, are never put in any other way."

Hmm. Might this long silence be something more than just silence? Might it contain a question that I need to hear? I pause again and listen. Silence. The sun is getting stronger while it inches closer to the ridge line. I ponder just what such a question might be. Another long pause. More silence. Profound silence. How long must I sit here before a "most pertinent question" reveals itself? Then a few squawks of a flicker. Is the bird trying to tell me something? I am beginning to feel that I am thinking way too hard as I try to figure out what this important question is.

In an instant, the thought occurs to me that, although I don't know what the question is, maybe the answers are all around me. The ancient granite and the lichens. The birds. The sky and the clouds and the sun. The weathered railing and the thought that eighty years, one month, and fifteen days ago, a few workers worked up here and probably sat right where I am now sitting. They enjoyed lunch while looking out at these same mountains, and maybe heard some of the same species of birds I've been hearing when they carved that date into some wet cement.

I imagine them as skinny young men, thankful to have the job of installing this railing, to do something worthwhile in the middle of the Great Depression. And suddenly they are right here with me. I can feel their presence. I can hear the sounds as they drilled holes into this hard rock and mixed the cement and cut the pipes. Their lives are long gone, yet they are still here in the fruits of their work that remain firmly cemented into this solid rock. I think of the hundreds of people I have brought here on countless guided hikes, and thousands of hikers before me, that leaned on this railing, that marveled at the view and the beauty and the peace of this place. I am filled with a feeling of immense gratitude for what those young men left here on this rocky point. They may be gone, but their good work remains.

Gratitude now becomes a part of my late afternoon experience at Lookout Point. And not only for the men that built this railing, but for the granite that I am perched upon, and the birds that punctuate the silence, and the sun that warms me. I am grateful for the thought-provoking writings of Henry David Thoreau, and my legs that brought me here, and for my ears that noticed the emphatic silence. And for the silence itself.

A small breeze is making me just cool enough to think about heading back down the trail. I can't say that the question hiding in the silence is any closer to being discovered. But it no longer matters. I put on my pack, and as I scramble up the rock towards the trail, I turn back and take another look at where I've been the last couple of hours. The sentiments of John Muir come to mind, "In every walk with Nature one receives far more than he seeks." Such a perfect summary of my afternoon hike to Lookout Point.

## Nature Education: The Heart of MPEC
*January 2015*

It will be fifteen years this February since MPEC first opened its doors in Pueblo Mountain Park's caretaker house. Anniversaries always bring with them opportunities to compare where we are and what we've become to where we were when things were just getting started. I recently found the rough draft of a document that I had written in the year prior to that February day in 2000 when MPEC officially opened its doors. It provides a look into the thinking that ultimately led to the creation of MPEC. Here are some excerpts from that document:

*The vision for why there is a Mountain Park Environmental Center is a citizenry that understands the basic components of a healthy natural environment, including the need for wild areas, places where ecological integrity is the primary management objective...a society where people enjoy and respect Nature, and take pride in living in a manner that is sustainable and compatible with a healthy natural environment. This vision is a society that considers the health of the natural environment (other species, all peoples, ecological relationships) in all its decisions.*

*The creation of such a citizenry is going to require many facets. Educating for such an ecologically literate society must be the foundation of such a societal change. In essence, such a society must be educated into existence. A vital component of such an education must involve providing opportunities for hands-on experiences in "wild Nature."*

*I see the Mountain Park Environmental Center's primary role in this process as providing programs where the community can access some of this education, with Pueblo Mountain Park as an ideal site for such experiential environmental education. Additionally, the organization will reach less mobile members of the community through other kinds of programs (e.g. lectures, workshops), occurring primarily in Pueblo Mountain Park.*

*Among those adults who have committed to advocating and working for the environment, it has been found that a common thread among them is very often childhood experiences where they could explore and "be" in Nature. Hence, an important part of MPEC programming will be providing such Nature-based experiences for children.*

At this fifteen-year juncture, it is clear to me that MPEC has stayed very much on course with this original vision. Sure, we have a lot more on our plate—we now manage and steward the 611-acre park, and we now run an overnight retreat center with our headquarters in the fully renovated Horseshoe Lodge. But, at the heart of why MPEC exists remains Nature education. The Lodge, the Park, the meals we serve in Arthur's Kitchen (named after the original visionary for Pueblo Mountain Park, Arthur Carhart), the buses and vans—it all rests on the foundation of connecting people with the natural world. If I was off, it was an under-estimation of just how much focus our programs would have on serving children. Bringing young people to Nature was always a fundamental part of MPEC's vision, but I did not envision just how many children we would get to work with each year.

Through the years, we have at times asked ourselves if this course is still the right one to be on? Is there still a need for Nature education? Are our programs relevant? Are we making a difference? Although it is clear—and sad—that we have not yet become "a society that considers the health of the natural environment in all its decisions," it also seems very clear that the need for such a societal mindset has probably never been greater. As for the value of connecting children to Nature, such discussions always lead me to the same answer: bringing children to Nature is absolutely good for the children. It is counterintuitive to think that these children will have a better chance of caring for Nature if they do not have the experiences they have through our programs, and which they would likely not have without MPEC.

An MPEC member recently sent this note:

> My husband just went to a foundation conference and the keynote speaker was Philippe Cousteau Jr. (who is carrying on the conservation work and legacy of his grandfather Jacques Cousteau). He said you would have enjoyed hearing him because he talked all about the kind of work MPEC is doing, and that the only way to make environmental changes is to educate children in outdoor education."

It remains as clear to me today as it did fifteen years ago—educating children is as important as ever! And the Mountain Park is an ideal place for that education to take place.

## I am Still in Love
*June 2, 2015*

After what turned out to be the wettest and chilliest month of May I can recall, today, the second day of June, feels like summer may just be on its way after all. It certainly is nice to see so much green, to hear the creek crashing over the rocks, and to smell the land verdant with moisture. I am ready for some summer weather.

To celebrate this momentous day of warmth and un-threatening skies, I set my feet onto the Northridge Trail and began a steady climb to the western top of the eroding granite batholith known as Devil's Canyon. After weeks of cool and cloudy days, these blue skies needed to be hiked under. And now here I sit, with Devil's Canyon and the rest of the park, the Beulah Valley as green as Ireland, Signal Mountain, the plains and the hazy eastern horizon comprising a most pleasing viewshed.

The soundtrack for my hike included several happy-sounding birds—spotted towhees, black-headed grosbeaks, mountain chickadees, and dark-eyed juncos, to name a few. I am not hearing many of them right now due to a fairly strong wind that is filling my ears with its hum. When the wind takes a break, the bird song returns. I can also hear the happy and excited voices of two groups of fifth-grade students from a Pueblo elementary school coming from the Mace and Tower Trails, both of which are across the canyon in the trees. Now and then I get a glimpse of the students, but it is their voices that make their presence known, expressing their pleasure in spending another day in this perfect outdoor classroom under these glorious blue skies. They are in the park for their final day of the Earth Studies program they've been participating in all school year, highlighted by a long hike to the Fire Tower as they learn about wildflowers and the basics of birdwatching.

All of these sounds—birds, wind, children—are music to my ears. Along with being such ideal habitat for so many species of birds, trees, wildflowers, and furry and scaly and squirmy creatures, the Mountain Park is such an ideal environment for learning about these fellow plants and animals with whom these students are sharing this little planet. It is my hope that, along with learning about all of this fascinating natural history, they are also learning a few things about themselves. As John Muir so aptly put it, "I only went out for a walk and finally concluded to stay out till sundown, for going out, I found, was really going in."

My hike today has given me the opportunity to do a bit of "going in" myself. What keeps coming to mind today as I take this hike, and sit on this ancient granite, and look out at the park that has been such a part of my life, is this powerful little poem by Gary Snyder: *Range after range of mountains / Year after year after year / I am still in love.*

These words say it all for me. My journey of creating MPEC has been so full of countless challenges—like hiking over

231

mountain range after mountain range, year after year after year. And yet, after all the ups and downs, I am still in love with what MPEC does—bring people, especially young people, to Nature. I still believe that connecting people with Nature is some of the most needed work to be done, here and everywhere. There are many more mountain ranges and years ahead, with so many more children who will need to hike and look at wildflowers and birds and shout out their joy through the trees. MPEC needs to be there to traverse those mountains so we can keep bringing people, young and not-so-young, to Nature, year after year after year.

## Autumn—A Time to Slow Down
*September 2, 2015*

It is quiet up here this morning. The squawk of a Clark's nutcracker, the clicking of a grasshopper, the chattering alarm of a pine squirrel, *chick-a-dee-dee-dee,* the unmistakable *yank* of a red-breasted nuthatch. I hear these sounds spread over several minutes, with utter quiet between. It still feels like summer on this hilltop a mile or so up a favorite trail. The air is quickly warming on its way into the 80s, as the weather report predicted.

None of the leaves have begun to put on their autumn colors yet, but the abundance of late summer wildflowers—sunspots, stiff goldenrod, smooth aster, Bahia ragleaf, Porter aster—clearly speaks of the imminent arrival of fall. The relative quiet does the same. Gone are melodious songs of birds in their breeding activity that seem to fill every audible space when the summer season is young. In place of all that ruckus are the occasional calls that I continue to hear as I sit, think and write. The wind just kicked up. It's a hot wind that reminds me that summer is still here. But it won't be long before the wind's message tells me that fall has arrived.

The lack of bird song, the mature late season wildflowers with few newly sprouted plants—these all reflect how the natural world slows down in the fall, in harmony with the natural rhythm of the seasons.

I've often reflected on how the human culture in which I live doesn't seem to do a whole lot of slowing down in the fall. Regardless of the season, our weeks are essentially the same "grind" that can feel quite endless. Sure, there is the break from school in the summer and a few weeks during the school year for children. But once a person steps into the adult world, the rhythm of our days and weeks is paced not by the seasons but by our jobs, technology, and the numerous demands that our modern culture expects of us. Except for a few holidays, illness, the week or two (or more if one is lucky) of vacation, or some extreme weather event—and even many of those days often result in little real slowing down—most of us never seem to get a chance to truly slow down, in the fall or at any other time of the year. Maybe it's just me, but it seems as if the pace of the human world just keeps getting faster and faster as the years go by. Slowing down in the fall? How quaint!

As a person who has always tried to stay connected to the natural world, I can't help but question whether we as individuals, and as a society, are missing out on something that we really shouldn't be missing by always being on the go. Instead, we continue on our seemingly ever-increasing pace that hardly seems to even notice the seasons beyond the inconveniences associated with inclement weather. Would we be healthier as individuals, and as a society, if our lives did reflect the rhythm of the seasons, and we did slow it down a notch or two in the fall?

As I ponder such questions, thoughts pop up about how such adjustments would impact our system of economics, a system that thrives on ever-increasing speed and growth. I suspect my thoughts would probably be considered blasphemous in the halls of our economic institutions.

Regardless, I still believe that much good would come out of choosing to live lives that more closely reflect the rhythm of the seasons. To paraphrase the great conservationist Aldo Leopold, we are much more than cogs in a system of economics. We are at core members of the ecological community that includes the soil, the water, the plants, the animals—and the seasons.

I, for one, am ready to slow down this fall. How about you?

## How Many More Autumns Do I Have Left?
*September 30, 2015*

*"The seasons come and go, summer follows spring and fall follows summer and winter follows fall, and human beings are born and mature, have their middle age, begin to grow older and die, and everything has its cycles. Day follows night, night follows day. It is good to be part of all of this."*
*~American Indian saying*

"One thing I want to do on this little getaway is walk in an aspen forest!" I said these words to Helene while leaving for a short getaway last week. As we drove our 1995 Eurovan west over the mountains, the colors of autumn were brilliantly alive as we headed towards a little lower elevation town on Colorado's western slope. I was pleased that we managed to carve out a few days from our busy lives, especially as we realized that the aspens up in the mountains we drove through were at peak color.

After a couple of glorious days filled with simple and delicious food, hot springs soaking, and hiking (in green conifer forests), some unforeseen circumstances necessitated we head for home sooner than we had planned. As we retraced our path back through Colorado's high country, I unhappily realized that my wish for a saunter among the golden aspens did not happen. While taking in the lovely fall scenery through the windshield of the van, I thought to myself, "How many more autumns will I get to experience before I am dead?" The late Steve Jobs once put it another way—how most things "just fall away in the face of death, leaving only what is truly important." Somewhere I heard that Buddhist philosophy says we have less time than we think.

Such thoughts led me to realize that this is my last autumn while in my 50s. "We may need to get home," I thought, "but it can wait just a little while longer." Taking that saunter in an aspen forest quickly became truly important. I found a little turnoff that led us to just what I was looking for. We were soon walking in the magic of an autumn aspen forest. The golden light seemed to be coming out of the leaves themselves as they percussively tinkled with the breeze. There is nothing quite like being in an aspen forest in its autumn glory!

I am not one to dwell on death and dying. But I am also not one who thinks that I am going to live to 110, and that my body will be able to do anything I want it to do right up until I'm 110. Life sure seems to be slipping by, and I have no idea if I have ten? twenty? thirty? forty? more autumns left. Or maybe this one is going to be my last. What I do know is that I am not going to live forever, and as hard as I try to keep my body healthy and strong, I know that this body of mine is not designed to go on forever. Bodies get old, and they eventually quit working. Until then, I plan on experiencing as many walks among the autumn aspens—and the winter, spring and summer aspens too—as I can.

## Sticking Around for Another Winter
*December 1, 2015*

Here I am—again! The last time I sat on this lichen-covered chunk of crumbling granite, it was a gentle spring afternoon. A handful of early season wildflowers, clumps of green grass, and a warm sun accompanied me that day. Fast forward several months to this early December day, and the plants are brown and dried up, their life energy pulled down into their roots to wait out the winter.

I've settled on a hillside that looks down on the park's upper road. This afternoon's sun is trying, unsuccessfully, to work its way through a thin cloud cover that has crept into the western sky. The sun was shining brightly earlier today and all day yesterday, melting most of the snow off this sloped sitting spot. So, I knew this place would be snowless—an ideal outdoor office to sit and write in an otherwise snowy winter landscape.

November ended only after fifteen inches of snow wrote the word *winter* all over the park. Clumps of snow remain on the hundreds of pine and fir trees that cover the north-facing slope directly in front of me. Tracks of snowshoers and cross-country skiers are visible down on the road, now closed off to motorized traffic, along with tracks showing the wanderings of the park's more hairy travelers—deer, rabbit, fox, squirrel. Clearly, there is still plenty of winter activity in the park.

This will be my fortieth winter in Beulah. After spending my first couple of decades of winters on the busy and noisy streets of New York City, I much prefer winters here in these Wet Mountains. I tried to leave Beulah once, in the fall before my seventh winter here, but my roots had already begun to stick, so here I am, ready for another winter. The western writer and environmentalist Wallace Stegner would call me a "sticker," someone who finds a place, settles, learns the place, and commits to it. As opposed to a "boomer," who is always looking for the next place to try and strike it rich. Being a sticker apparently works for me. I like the way poet and environmentalist Gary Snyder put it, "Find your place on the planet, dig in, and take responsibility from there."

In the last two weeks, I learned that two people I've known who were about my age will not be experiencing this winter, or any winter, again. Life can be so short! I have no idea how many more winters I will get to live here in Beulah, or get to live through at all. What I do know is that I intend on savoring every bit of this winter, to live each day of it to its fullest.

The sound of a clump of snow falling off a branch and landing on a large rock—like a hissing sound or tiny pebbles hitting a hard surface—pulls my eyes from the page of my journal to the winter landscape that is quickly *feeling* more and more winter-like. I can make out the position of the sun through the gray—it is moments away from reaching the horizon. As always seems to happen when the winter sun drops below the western ridge, the temperature drops as well, and quickly. It is about time I slip on my snowshoes, add my tracks to the ones down on the road, and get some warm blood pumping around my body.

Cold! Snow! Ice! Wind! Bring them on—I am thrilled to be a sticker in this southern Colorado valley, and thrilled to still have another winter to be alive in!

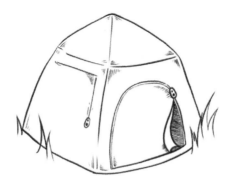

**Turning Sixty on a Redrock Wilderness Retreat**
*March 2016*

## *DAY ONE*

The clock in the car reads 6:21 as I pull out of my morning driveway and head down the dirt road. Destination: Elephant Canyon, Utah! I listen to NPR as I work my way south towards I-25, and then west on US160. Presidential candidates Donald Trump, Bernie Sanders, Marco Rubio, Hillary Clinton, and Ted Cruz seem to monopolize the news stories. Especially Donald Trump. I climb La Veta Pass and am happy to lose reception. Enough of Donald.

I leave Cortez, Colorado on Hwy 491 and immediately see the snowy La Sal Mountains directly in front of me, probably 75 miles away as the raven flies. An island of white floating on a red dirt sagebrush landscape. I pass through Dove Creek, "Home of the Anasazi Beans," and soon cross the Colorado/Utah state line. I approach the town of Monticello and see that a wind farm has sprouted just north of town since the last time I drove this highway a year or so ago. As I lose elevation heading north on US191, signs of the red rock country I am heading towards in Canyonlands National Park start to peak out from between the green pinyons and junipers.

I arrive at the Needles District Visitor Center at 2:30—eight hours in the car. My left sciatic, which turns 60 today, doesn't like it one bit, being in the car for that long. A short and pleasant visit with the ranger, a quick late lunch, and I am soon hoisting my backpack onto my back. Not since I finished the Colorado Trail a couple of years ago has my body felt this familiar combination of sensations—the weight of the pack balancing between hips and shoulders, hip flexors saying "hello," and that feeling that borders on euphoria, knowing I am going to spend a few days immersed in what Gary Snyder calls "wild Nature." This wild redrock canyon country very much qualifies as wild Nature!

This four-day adventure is a pilgrimage of sorts. I first came to canyon country about 25 years ago after hearing about it from a magazine article about the quietest places in the country. Being a passionate appreciator of natural quiet, I took note of the Needles District of Canyonlands National Park. As soon I could make it happen, I made my way to southeast Utah. I was accompanied by my two kids, Sierra, age 13 and Sequoia, age 10; Todd, a good friend of mine and his daughter Sarah, age 12; and Dylan, a good friend of and the same age as Sequoia. We arrived at the same Elephant Hill Trailhead I just arrived at and was heading for the same EC2 campsite that I am hiking to today. That first trip here forever imprinted this landscape deep into me. I've been back to what has become my favorite National Park nearly every year since that iconic first backpack into redrock canyon country—car camping, backpacking, day hiking, river rafting. I've been here in rain, hellish summer heat, snow, wind, and days just like today—warm, sunny, gentle. But I've never experienced this place solo.

The seed to come here on my own was planted exactly a decade ago, the day I turned 50. I was on a solo backpack along Frijoles Canyon in New Mexico's Bandelier National Monument to say good-bye to my 40s and welcome my 50s. I decided then that, when I turn 60, I would acknowledge that milestone—which sounded a good long decade away—on another solo wilderness retreat, in Canyonlands National Park.

Well, that decade has come and, as of today, it has officially gone. Here I am, just where I said I'd be when I turn 60. All too often, we make plans to do something for ourselves, but life gets in the way, or we let life get in the way, and those plans fall through. I'm guilty of it. But not this time; backpack on my back, sun on my face, I'm a just-turned-60-year-old pilgrim happily working my way into the backcountry of Canyonlands.

\* \* \*

I arrive at the campsite, set up the tent, and head down to where there should be a good source of water. This canyon country is a desert, so finding water can be tricky. It's been a rather wet winter in this part of the world (thanks to this year's strong El Nino, that warm water in the eastern equatorial Pacific Ocean thousands of miles away from this place), so the "puddle" I've found water in many times in the past is bigger than I've ever seen it. In fact, there is more water along this wash than I've ever seen. Good, finding water will not be a problem.

Dinner heartily enjoyed and cleaned up for the night, the evening sky is graced by a just-past-new sliver of a moon, sliding down into a gap in the backlit hoodoos that make up the western horizon. I locate the Big Dipper, standing on its handle, of which its last star is hidden behind the rocks that rise from across the main canyon. The sky begins to explode with stars. I check the time—7:29. Hmm—nights are long on late winter backpacks. I'm glad I brought along something to read—a copy of *Desert Solitaire*, Edward Abbey's classic book about this redrock country—Abbey's country.

I can still see all of us on that first trip here, listening to *Desert Solitaire*. We were preparing dinner one evening, the fading light of the day just barely discernible in the western sky. Sierra was reading aloud, the book illuminated by her headlamp. Everyone, even Dylan, who really liked to talk, was quiet, listening. Sierra was sitting on a log, knees bent, feet out in front, reading away, while a mouse scampered back and forth right underneath her legs. No one else noticed. I said nothing, as I figured she wouldn't have appreciated knowing that little critter was as close as it was.

When we turned in for the night, we all decided to sleep out under the stars, lined up side- by-side-by-side across the slickrock. Haley's comet was a part of the magical desert night sky for a few weeks that early spring, which was off to our front left as we lay there on our slickrock bed. I can close my eyes and see the bunch of us all those years ago, cozy in our sleeping bags on the same white slickrock where I ate dinner this evening. Sometime in the middle of the night, Sequoia, who was next to me, whispers, "Dad, are you awake?" "Yeah." "A mouse just ran over my head," he said in a rather nonchalant voice. "Are you ok?" "Yeah." "Then don't worry about it, it won't hurt you. Go back to sleep." "Ok. Good night." "Good night," I whispered, "see you in the morning."

## DAY TWO

I slept cold and poorly last night. The slow leak in the air mattress, which eventually eliminated the insulating layer of air between me and the cold rock underneath, might have had something to do with it. I was happy to see the light of the new day through the walls of the tent. Tonight I think I'll huff and puff a middle-of-the-night refill and see if that helps.

I decide to warm my slowly waking body by exploring around camp. Surrounded by slabs of slickrock poised at every angle, I scramble up some red sandstone that leads to a slab of white sandstone, and then another and another. My body now wide awake, it feels good to be warm. Oatmeal and hot tea finish the job. As if that isn't enough, the sun slips up over the rock wall to the east and soon has me shedding a layer.

After hiking back down Elephant Canyon the way I came up yesterday afternoon, I reach a trail intersection sign after about a mile. Chesler Park: 1.0 m. I've hiked many of the trails in the Needles District, but this trail to Chesler Park is one I haven't done. I climb out of the main canyon through a side canyon filled with a tortured hodgepodge of broken rocks, boulders, and an assortment of desert plants, some of which I can readily identify—Utah juniper, Fremont's mahonia, pinyon pine, dwarf mountain mahogany. It may still be winter, but I come across a few early spring wildflowers in blossom here and there—western wallflower, Newberry's twinpod. I've never seen a flash flood here in the park, but I've read about them and know that they can make a real mess of these drainages. Make them look like this chaotic mix of earth, stone and hardy plants through which my morning trail travels. It does make for fun hiking though.

I reach a high point and turn around to a spectacular sight that I've seen from other trails that I never grow tired of. Those same snowy La Sals that I saw while driving yesterday look even more stunning with a foreground dominated by the red and white striped spires that give the Needles District its name. It is all the more pleasing to see, not through the windshield of a car, but from the heart of this wild landscape that can only be reached on foot. I suppose one of the reasons I wanted to do a wilderness backpacking retreat for my 60<sup>th</sup> was to see if my body could still do it—enjoy hiking these slickrock up and down trails with a pack on my back. I admit I am feeling a bit sore, as I haven't backpacked in a while, but beyond that, I feel great and I'm having a blast!

I hike into the grassy Chesler Park, named after a horse rancher who operated in the area long ago. The day is soft and warm while I notice some patches of snow lingering on a north-facing slope off in the distance. I work my way through the Joint Trail, which is a series of narrow slot canyons, in places less than two feet wide where I have to remove my pack and turn sideways to get through. I am now planted on a slab of white slickrock that is decorated with black, white, grey, and a few tiny yellow lichens. In a miniature crevice of rocky pink soil grows a small lomatium in bloom, its tiny lemon-colored blossoms saying that spring is, indeed, on its way. A high ceiling of thin clouds is weakening the sunshine, but the solar energy absorbed by the rock is keeping me warm. I watch a couple of chipmunks scurry over the rocks across the wash. They both jump into a just-greening shrub and seem to disappear. Oh, there they go, back across the rock and out of sight.

Time to begin working my way back to camp—about three easy miles from where I sit. The songs of a Say's phoebe and a mountain bluebird accompany my own singing as I lazily work my way back to camp. *Nobody knows how we got to the top of the hill / But since we're on our way down / we might as well enjoy the ride....* I suppose that if I needed a theme song for how I feel turning 60, these lyrics from James Taylor's *Secret O' Life* work pretty well. Of course, 60 is a ways beyond the top of the hill, but whether I am 60%, 75%, or 98% through my life, I so want to enjoy the rest of the ride. This sentiment is another reason why I am here on this little wilderness retreat in this favorite place of mine. As it's been said, it's later than you think!

Back to camp by mid-afternoon, the clouds have thickened, but the day is still mild and gentle. After hiking around seven miles, it feels good to shed my hiking shoes and just hang out at camp. It sometimes feels as if my life over the past several decades has had so little of this extended kind of unstructured, undistracted, unpreoccupied quiet time to slow way down and just be. I have with me the most recent issue of *High Country News*, a special issue devoted to our National Park System, which turns 100 this year. What a great creation, National Parks. That I have this wild place in which to retreat for solitude, reflection and wilderness immersion is one of the greatest benefits of being an American citizen. Our system of National Parks is very high on my list of what makes this a great nation.

\* \* \*

I've never been much of a meditator, at least in the manner that meditation is often portrayed—sitting still, focusing on breath, keeping the mind free from extraneous thoughts. I have gone through stretches of days, maybe a few weeks, when I meditated in this fashion. But it would never last. I just returned from the backcountry ritual of finding and filtering water. This necessary backcountry practice here in the desert, a form of meditation that works well for me, always goes like this: I mindfully approach the water source and find the best place to position myself, careful not to disturb the water with additional stones, sand, sticks or anything a careless foot could kick into it. These desert water holes are usually harboring a fair share of insects (both dead and alive), maybe a surface covering of something slimy, silt settled at the bottom… disturbing it only adds to what the filter needs to remove.

Properly positioned, I am careful not to accidentally drop the filter or any parts of it into the water, except the end of the tube designed to be in the source of unfiltered water. Screwing this process up could result in contracting some sort of intestinal bug that could ruin a trip, or worse. With the end of each tube where it is supposed to be, I slowly pump—about 50 pumps per liter. No way to rush the process, as the filter can only handle a small amount of water per stroke. Slow, methodical, focused—kind of like meditation. Plus, the opportunity to gaze at the surroundings, which is always a pleasure, and absorb the music of the wildness that surrounds me. Three and a half liters filtered, plus a nice deep watering of my own parched self, I then carefully drain the filter and place it in its carrying case, ready for my next water meditation.

*   *   *

Why solo? Why come out here by myself? I was struggling with this question yesterday. A subtle taste of uneasiness accompanied me as I left the Elephant Hill trailhead, leaving the car and the road and civilization behind, and began hiking into this wild place. It wasn't a fear of wild animals—even though I had seen a poster back at the Visitor Center: *Warning! A mountain lion has recently been seen in the Elephant Hill area.* I've hiked thousands of miles in wild places, sometimes not necessarily at the top of the food chain, and I always take with me a strong belief in John Muir's adage that a wilderness feared is a wilderness lost. But I do bring a healthy dose of respect for these wild animals.

So, it wasn't fear. It may have had something to do with feeling like I was doing something wrong. Somewhere, maybe as a boy scout, I was told that traveling alone in the wilds is dangerous. A friend questioned why I would want to spend my birthday by myself in the desert, away from the people I love and that love me (I did have a little celebration with my wife, daughter and grandkids a few days before I left). My aging mom is not well, my daughter is crazy-busy with nursing school and can always use my help with the grandkids, and so I am certainly needed back home. And there I was, walking away from all of that. Am I being selfish? Whatever the cause, it was nagging at me. Not big, but still there.

As today wore on, I could feel the uneasiness dissolving as the red rock landscape worked its way into me (and onto me, as this red dirt has a way of finding every part of me to take a ride on). As I sauntered alone along desert trails, I thought of the numerous treks I've done in this park with many combinations of people. I began to recognize that the experience of being out here on my own has a different texture, a different flow, compared to being here with others. Not that I don't love being here with others—I do. I love sharing this magical place. And, admittedly, I have had some moments out here this time when I wished I was here with my wife, kids, grandkids, friends. But this solo texture is now feeling like a good thing for me to be experiencing at this little blink of time in my life. Retreating into these wild canyons for a few days of solitude, with extended time to ponder, reflect, not talk, write, and be guided only by my own whims and wants, is feeling more and more like I am doing something right. Again,

I think of John Muir, "...for going out, I found, was really going in."

* * *

The cloudy afternoon has given way to one last show from the sun, shining through a narrow gap between the clouds and the western horizon, illuminating the very top of the sandstone wall to the east. It looks like the light is coming not from the sun but out of the uppermost part of the redrock wall itself. And then, in a matter of seconds, the light dissolves and the evening becomes several notches darker. A canyon wren sounds like it is rehearsing its iconic canyon song of descending notes. Another bird whose song I am not familiar with adds some counterpoint to the wren. Dueling birds! The thin cloud cover above the eastern wall is now blushed with a peachy pink, once again brightening up the evening landscape. As I watch it becomes brighter. The color reveals that the clouds are moving to the north as they become brighter still against a backdrop of a bluish gray sky. I couldn't ask for a better evening show!

I turn my gaze behind me and see that the western sky is just as alive with color. Feathery clouds of pink drift over the Needles on the northwest horizon, the rock's red and white stripes still visible in the fading light. The evening show has many acts; just when I think it is over, another colorful act begins. The birds have quieted and the deep silence of the canyon, of the park, of the Universe fills my ears. Fills my entire self. Oh, it was a long drive getting here, but this, all by itself, makes it well worth it. The latest act is fading slowly, as if the silence is sucking the color right out of the sky.

Ah, the next act, stage west—the crescent sliver of moon, a

shallow U facing almost directly up, is coming through the thinning clouds. Next, depending on the cloud cover, will be the stars. Will I ever get to sleep tonight?


## *DAY THREE*

Except for some gusty winds that woke me several times, I had a warmer and better sleep last night. I climb out of the tent to a cloudless, desert blue sky. Oatmeal, nuts and tea are my fuel for a hike that, at this moment, I am not sure how far will be. I start up the wash where I get my water and continue until I reach an unpassable pass were it not for the two ladders the Park Service has conveniently provided. Without them, it would be a quick mile hike to a fifteen-foot vertical wall at the top of the canyon, then back the way I came. Instead, I climb up and over and eventually into another drainage—Big Spring Canyon.

At a high point on the slickrock, I have the choice of turning around for a four-mile out-and-back hike or continue forward and make an eight-mile loop of today's trek. The day is young, I am feeling rather young myself (I *am* only 60, after all) and a lot less sore than yesterday, and the clouds that were building a little while ago have melted away. I know of a truly gorgeous spot along this loop, a shaded pool, an oasis in this desert, a great place to eat lunch. Onward!

Interesting that this rock is called slickrock, as it is quite the opposite of slick. My shoes seem to stick to the abrasive sandstone, even on steep sections. Off the unslick slickrock now, my hike through Big Spring Canyon is wetter than I've ever seen it. It must have been a *very* wet winter, as there are few places along the two-mile drainage where water is not in sight. This is a far cry from the many times I've been here with nary a puddle anywhere. The day is warming in spite of chilly gusts that seem to say, "Hey, spring, not so fast—notice the date on the calendar? It is still winter!"

Up and over into another expanse of slickrock punctuated by pinyons and junipers, I arrive at the hidden mini-pond feeling pangs of hunger. Perfect timing! I enjoy lunch serenaded by the music of water constantly dripping into the pool from a seep in the rock. Unlike Big Spring Canyon, I've never seen this hidden place empty of water. Roughly thirty feet in diameter and who knows how deep, the pool is mostly shaded by a white sandstone overhang. A few cottonwoods, still in their winter leaflessness, grow nearby. I look beyond this hidden wet spot to the landscape I just hiked through—pleasant today but sun-baked hot and bone-dry for many months of the year. I am sure this pool is well known to the locals—bobcats, coyotes, mountain lions, foxes, mule deer...

\* \* \*

I am glad to be back at camp after a perfect day of hiking. According to the map, I hiked an 8.6-mile loop. I didn't encounter any more ladders, but there was a weathered gray log with notches cut into it, leaning on a huge boulder, that provided access into a tunnel-like, hundred-foot-long slot in the rock that opened up into the upper reaches of Big Spring Canyon. This park is aptly named—Canyonlands! I must say, hiking here is a delight. It has it all: wooded trails—not deep forest woods, but a few tall cottonwoods among scrubby woods of oak, juniper and pinyon; top-of-the-world slickrock hiking; an assortment of wildflowers—even this early in the warm season, a few species are already in bloom, with many more to follow; at least one mountain lion—which I've never seen a sign of; and out-of-this-world beauty every step of the way.

Of course, it is hardly out of this world—it is very much a part of this world. And, thanks to a man who loved this wild desert landscape, it is a protected part of this world that has been set aside as a place where people can step away from our increasingly fast-paced society, for a day, a week, a month. Bates Wilson began lobbying for the creation of Canyonlands National Park in the early 1960s. He convinced Secretary of the Interior Steward Udall that this canyon country should become a part of the nation's system of National Parks, and in 1964 President Johnson signed it into law. The park has grown in size since those early years, and exists so people can experience its solitude, its rugged wildness, its beauty, and so the ecological processes that take place within its boundaries can go about their business protected from our society's heavy footprint that continues to have such an impact on so much of the rest of the country's lands.

A large majority of Americans believe that our nation's public lands, such as this park, are a good thing. But not everyone. Just a few weeks ago, a handful of armed militants who believe that federal ownership and management of such lands is not a good thing illegally took over the Malheur National Wildlife Refuge in Oregon. They occupied it for five weeks, damaged parts of it, calling for the federal government to turn over public lands to local control. Right now, while I sit on this slickrock under this desert sky, those individuals are sitting in jail. Where they should be, as far as I'm concerned.

Yes, most of my fellow citizens and I fully support the idea of National Parks and public lands. But there are those who would rather these wild places be used not for recreation, education, and preservation of natural values and processes, but opened up for more mining, grazing, logging and other extractive uses. We who love these lands must remain ever vigilant, as there are those who want nothing less than to undo the efforts of Bates Wilson and so many others that worked tirelessly to protect wild sanctuaries like this amazing park. Thank you, Bates Wilson, wherever you are (in so many ways, you are right here with me).

\* \* \*

I visually explore the red-and-white spires, hundreds of feet tall, which rise from the canyon floor directly across from camp. How long have they been there? I am sure they looked exactly the same eight or nine hundred years ago, when the Indigenous peoples that lived in these canyons painted the pictographs that I was admiring on a canyon wall not far from where I am sitting here at camp. There may have been some different plants growing here 12,000 years ago, when the climate was wetter and cooler, and humans first began to cultivate plants and animals for food halfway around the world, but I bet these sandstone spires looked pretty much the same even then. Geologists say these rock formations of Cedar Mesa Sandstone were originally dunes of wind-blown sand and flood-eroded sediments that formed over 200 million years ago. Twenty million years ago, other forces began to fracture the solidified dunes. Millions of years of erosion by wind and water worked those cracks and fractures into the sculpted pillars that I am looking at now, on this late winter 2016 evening, two days into my 61st year.

There is a feeling of, what is it—silliness? absurdity?—to sit among these ancient rocks and reflect upon my briefer-than-brief 60 years of being alive on this planet. Then again, the short little speck of time that is my life is all I've got. It brings up a range of feelings to be here at this time in the middle of this magnificent landscape—humbled, joyous, inspired, awe, insignificant. I sit as quietly as the canyon is on this late afternoon. Lines from a Mary Oliver poem that I've been trying to memorize emerge out of the quiet:

> Tell me, what else should I have done?
> Doesn't everything die at last, and too soon?
> Tell me, what is it you plan to do
> with your one wild and precious life?

One wild and precious life. Hmm. One. Wild. Precious. Life. I can't think of a better place in which to contemplate my one wild and precious life. One thing I know is that I want more wildness in this precious life of mine. And I know I am right where I need to be today.

Yes, from one angle, my life can seem small and insignificant in the face of this ancient stone. Then I am reminded of how the life of a high school dropout, a dryland cowboy, was able to convince the Washington DC power brokers to get behind this crazy idea of making a National Park out of this God-forsaken landscape, as many people considered this place. I suppose Bates Wilson could have looked at his smalltime, western cowboy life as never being able to have much of an impact beyond his little red dirt world. Fortunately for the rest of us, and for this magical landscape, he didn't.

When considered against the geologic time represented in these rocks, I suspect that what Wilson or any of us accomplish will probably always seem like a speck of meaningless dust. But, when considered within the realm of our country's history, the foreseeable future of this land, and a good many handfuls of human generations, Wilson's efforts are hugely significant. It's a bit of a paradox, how being here can conjure up feelings of insignificance, which can be disempowering. But if applied appropriately, that feeling of insignificance can lead to humility, perspective, not taking oneself too seriously...all good things— for individuals, for a society, for our species.

Being here can lead to empowerment—empowerment that comes from meeting the physical challenges associated with getting around this place, or the psychological challenges that a few days of wilderness solitude can provoke. Being here can also lead to a sense of hope, something that often seems, at least to me, pretty hard to come by as the 21$^{st}$ century unfolds. Along with a capacity for so much destruction, greed, and disregard for so much and so many, the fact that this little corner of the planet has been deliberately set aside as a place protected from ourselves—a place where we actually choose to put limits on what we *could* do to this place, but choose not to—is a reason for hope. Yes, we as a people are capable of self-restraint, and that makes me feel hopeful.

\* \* \*

The sun sets while I take a leisurely stroll up-canyon. Unlike last evening, the sky is completely cloud-free tonight. The wind has diminished to a few gusty breezes. The air does feel much colder than it did the last two nights. Maybe I will wear an extra layer tonight. Without any clouds, the slightly larger sliver of moon is desert-sky clear as the evening slowly begins to darken. Still no stars. Soon!

I plan on rising early for a quick start to what will be a long day. The hike out of here will be the pleasant part. Sorry sciatic— we have that same drive to do in the opposite direction tomorrow. As quick as it started, my wilderness retreat to say good-bye to my 50s and hello to my 60s will soon be over. But it's not over yet! On the many hikes I've guided over the years, I would often say to my group of hikers towards the end that the best part of the hike—like some cool animal sighting, or something unexpected—could still be ahead of us. The same holds true right now—I still have a night to spend in this amazing desert wilderness, plus what I expect to be a very pleasant early morning hike. Who knows what will happen!


## *DAY FOUR*


Up at first light, I break camp as the canyon slowly becomes day. I am on the trail as the first rays of sunlight hit the upper walls of the canyon. As I hike these last few miles, I am filled with a great sense of energy and lightness. Yes, my pack is a bit lighter, having eaten most of the food I packed in, but that's not really the reason for this feeling. Sixty feels pretty darn good if you ask me!

Quiet, silence, peacefulness, stillness—these words all come to mind as I hike down and then out of Elephant Canyon on this early morning. They are more than just descriptive of this desert morning—they *are* this place, as much as these rocks are this place. I stop often to just drink it all in. There are stretches when there is *no* sound at all—no bird song, no wind, no jets (halleluiah), nothing at all. Then a spotted towhee sings its chattering song and I can't help but feel like I am in heaven. It was Thoreau who said that heaven is under our feet as well as over our heads. He would have found confirmation of that here with me this morning. I think he would agree that heaven is also found sandwiched between the ground beneath and the sky above, right here in the perfect stillness of a redrock desert morning.

\* \* \*

As I drive out of the Elephant Hill parking lot, window down, I hear the song of a canyon wren and I can't help but smile. This little bird is the voice, the *spokesbird,* of these Canyonlands. I've heard the song a thousand times, but this morning, as I make my way out of the park, it's as if the song is being sung just for me. Is the canyon saying something to me? If so, what? I have my ideas, but I can't really say I know for sure just what this land might be saying. I suppose that maybe, if I keep coming back to this redrock land of wild canyons, I'll figure it out in my 60s. Sounds like a good plan to me. I'll be back!

## Forever Thankful for Parks
*March 2016*

I've heard the park referred to as Pueblo State Park, Beulah Mountain Park, and Pueblo National Park, among others. These 611 acres of forests, shrublands, the meandering path of South Creek, and an amazing canyon comprised of 200-million-year-old granite is correctly known as Pueblo Mountain Park. It is not owned by the State of Colorado, so it is not a state park, nor by the United States, so it is not a National Park. It is located in Beulah, so it is understandable that some might call it Beulah Mountain Park, but since it is owned by the City of Pueblo, it is Pueblo Mountain Park. Since 2008, the City has contracted with the nonprofit Mountain Park Environmental Center to manage the park for the City.

In 2020 we will celebrate the park's 100-year anniversary—it was on January 15, 1920 that the City purchased the park, at a cost of $6,000. Speaking of anniversaries and parks, this year marks the 100-year anniversary of the National Park Service. In the decades leading up to 1916, our nation had already established 35 National Parks and Monuments, starting with Yellowstone in 1872. But there was no cohesive management of these parks—administering to them was done by the Forest Service (part of the Department of Agriculture), the War Department, or the Department of Interior. Lacking unified management, many of these parks and monuments suffered from lack of funding and protection from private commercial interests that saw in these lands lots of dollar signs through exploitation in one form or another.

Reminiscent of the philosophical battles that took place when the creation of the US Forest Service was being debated 15 years earlier, there were those that promoted a utilitarian approach to managing these park lands (an approach ultimately adopted by the Forest Service), while others believed that preservation should be the guiding principle. Stephen Mather, a wealthy industrialist with a strong conservation ethic, championed the preservationist philosophy and the establishment of a strong, separate federal agency to carry it out. Mather was ultimately successful—on August 15, 1916, while Europe was embroiled in the ravages of World War I, President Woodrow Wilson signed the Organic Act, establishing the National Park Service (NPS). Mather became the NPS's first director with the mandate of protecting the parks "unimpaired for the enjoyment of future generations."

I doubt that President Wilson or the National Park Service's early supporters could have envisioned how the system of National Parks would grow to what it is today—a vast network of 408 parks, monuments, and other sites that have become some of the most visited tourism destinations in the world, as well as some of the most vitally important lands in ecosystem and wildlife preservation. In 1920, National Parks saw one million visitors; two years ago, 292.8 million people visited National Park system sites, generating $27 billion in economic activity.

Each of America's National Parks—what author and conservationist Wallace Stegner called "the best idea we ever had"—was the result of a relatively small number of people who had a vision, and then committed to seeing that vision become reality. Against steep odds and powerful business interests, they fought, and they won; their vision is why our nation's greatest natural treasures now belong to everyone and remain preserved forever. Of course, as those of us in the conservation field know all too well, any wins in protecting the natural world are never truly "forever"—there will always be new threats or old threats resurfacing, and this includes threats to the integrity and health of the National Park Service and our National Parks and Monuments.

America's system of National Parks has influenced nations around the world to create their own National Parks. I can't help but wonder if the vision to create Pueblo Mountain Park was also influenced by the establishment of the National Park Service. Is it a coincidence that a few years after the NPS was created, a group of Pueblo-area visionaries and the energetic Forest Service employee Arthur Carhart created a local Mountain Park? Wild, scenic, natural—was Pueblo Mountain Park initially inspired by the recent National Park story? Yes or no, all of us are now the beneficiaries of the vision of these inspired people. Thanks to their fortitude and hard work, there are national—and state and local—parks, preserving natural and cultural wonders that belong to not just the few and the wealthy, but to all citizens. I'm with Stegner—I believe our parks are one of the best ideas we ever had!

\* \* \*

Postscript
*February 2023*

Recent years have shed much light on our country's less-than-admirable, and often horrific treatment of certain groups of people, including this land's Native peoples. A more complete history of how our National Parks and other public lands came to be must include the fact that before they could become public lands, they often needed to be cleared of Indigenous peoples, usually through dishonest negotiations and violence.

Of course, this story of eliminating Native Americans from what ultimately became our National Parks is essentially just one chapter in how the United States in its entirety came to be. Our nation's expansion was based on the belief in manifest destiny, that white Europeans were divinely ordained to spread across the entire North American continent, doing whatever was necessary to remove any obstacles, including Indigenous peoples.

This story of a people or country or empire conquering other peoples and nations and dispossessing them of their land is a part of the human story that has been repeated numerous times around the world. But knowing that fact does not, from my perspective, lessen the wrongness of how that same cruel story is how my own nation came to be. What was done to Indigenous peoples in order to create the United States of America, including its National Parks, was wrong.

So, where does that leave a supporter, user and deep admirer of our public lands? How do I reconcile my continued use of our National Parks and other public lands—in fact, my use of all places of these United States—with the fact that these lands were violently and dishonestly stolen from its Indigenous inhabitants? That is a question I may never feel I can adequately answer, but it is a question I will continue to try to find answers to. In my view, the first step in expanding one's understanding of something is to acknowledge the need for that expansion. I believe that I would be remiss in my responsibility as a citizen of this country, and as a person committed to learning and always being open to expanding and growing my understanding of things, to not acknowledge this dark side of the story of our National Parks.

## The Transformation of a Mountain Park Icon
*May 31, 2016*

The song of a black-headed grosbeak fills the air with its gloriously happy song. Even the occasional loud gust of wind cannot silence the beauty of its song. Swallows flit here and there below a mostly cloudy sky on this cool last day of May. When the grosbeak pauses—to catch its breath?—my ears catch the song of another grosbeak up the hill. There's the melancholy song of a hermit thrush. And a dusky flycatcher. And a spotted towhee. I love these songs!

With my back comfortably leaning against a neighboring pine, my eyes are closely examining the current condition of the park's famous "leaning tree," a ponderosa pine that has been greeting hikers at the start of the Tower Trail for many years. The former condition of this iconic tree of the Mountain Park has been a topic of many conversations, questions, and guided hikes. The tree's hefty trunk leaned at about a forty-five-degree angle for fifteen feet or so, before it turned towards the sky for another fifty feet. That it could remain standing at such an angle, supporting so much weight, seemed to defy gravity. It was a wonder of Nature and a true icon of the park.

Many of us who have spent much time in Pueblo Mountain Park have become rather fond of the "leaning tree." This tree has meant different things to different people. We've climbed it, taken pictures of it, appreciated its unique beauty, wondered how it got that way, marveled at how it seemed to ignore the laws of physics to remain upright at such an angle.

If there is one constant in Nature, it is that nothing remains the same. Causes include floods, fire, cold, ice, lightning, birth, aging, death—a multitude of causes, but everything changes. The list also includes heavy wet snow, typical of springtime in the Rockies. And it was such a wet snow this past April that brought about a life-ending change to this leaning ponderosa pine tree that lived its long, interesting life at the trailhead of the Tower Trail.

I scan the yellow wood which is now exposed where the tree split. The tree's position on the ground tells me that it rolled to the south as it fell. Above the split trunk is a hodge-podge of the tree's broken branches mixed with branches from a nearby tree it hit as it went down. It must have been quite a sight, and sound, when this tree came crashing down. I think of the silly question, "If a tree falls in the forest and no one is there to hear it, does it make a sound?" Such species arrogance, as if natural phenomena—in this case, the sound of a falling tree—require the presence of a human for it to occur. As far as I am aware, no person was here to witness its fall. Yet I am sure it was a spectacular sound, lasting only a few seconds, only to return the forest to the soft whisper of falling snow.

All living things eventually die—including iconic trees. It took the additional weight of a heavy spring snow to tip the scale towards just a little too much weight for its angled trunk to support—and to tip the scale towards the tree's death.

The decision has been made to re-route a small section of trail so the fallen tree can remain right where it is. Over the next many decades, this tree that has meant so much to so many will continue to change as natural processes slowly transform the tree back into the soil from which it grew. It may no longer be a living organism, but this tree that has been telling many stories for many years will continue to tell stories. To hear them, all a person has to do is spend an hour, or a morning, or a day here at the Tower Trailhead, sit down with your back against a nearby tree, be quiet and still—and listen.

## The Circle Time Parade of Changes
*August 25, 2016*

I am walking through a vanilla forest. A sunny, humid morning after a couple of rainy days has filled the air, and my nostrils, with the natural sweet aroma of the ponderosa pines. There is also a hint of coolness in the breeze that is tugging on the warmth of the sunshine, most welcome after the hot and dry summer that is winding down. I am glad I brought along a jacket.

Everything about the landscape through which the trail climbs tells me that the change of the seasons is underway, and we will soon see this summer slip into fall. Apparently Earth is still revolving around the sun. It's been a pretty dismal summer for wildflowers due to the lack of rain. The few flowers that are in bloom—stiff goldenrod, hairy golden aster, Kansas gayflower, Porter aster, smooth aster (all members of the Sunflower Family, typical of late summer)—are right on schedule to welcome in the fall season. The pink and white kinnikinnick flowers of last spring have all become crimson berries about the size of a large pea. They will turn brown as the fall takes hold, unless the bears get to them first—kinnikinnick is also called bearberry, since bears purportedly like to eat them.

There is no birdsong to fill the vanilla air, as breeding season for the park's feathered travelers is over for 2016. Yet, for a late morning in late summer, the birds seem especially active and vocal. Steller's jays, mountain chickadees, spotted towhees, western wood peewees, and several others that I can't quite identify are filling the cool air with their calls and squawks—but not their songs.

I am pleased, and a bit surprised considering how dry it's been, to see the oaks carrying a fairly healthy crop of acorns. Acorns are rich in carbohydrates, protein and fat; hence, they are an important fall food for wild turkeys, squirrels, chipmunks, bear, and deer. Some recent new residents of the park, acorn woodpeckers, are so fond of acorns that they store them in small holes that they drill into trees. The large pine snag that is just west of the parking lot at the Horseshoe Lodge is a favorite tree of these clown-like birds. I just walked by that tree a little while ago and, sure enough, I heard the acorn woodpecker's distinctive call. Since being spotted during a Guided Birding Hike I led a few years ago, a small population has established itself in the park, an indication that acorn woodpeckers are moving north from New Mexico as the climate warms.

As I hike out of the pines and into a rocky open section of trail, I see that the mountain mahogany is also carrying a good seed crop. Many birds and small mammals eat the nutritious seeds, conspicuous due to their white, feathery, spiral attachments that seem to cover the branches of this small shrub.

Yes, all of this is the land saying loud and clear—fall is on its way!

Hmm, a raindrop. And another. And another. The sunshine

has given way to clouds, which are now beginning to shed some rain. It looks like there will be at least three consecutive days of rain as August nears its final days. Maybe this dry summer will go out on a wet note. Maybe it will be a wet fall—rain to start, and some nice, wet snow too. And maybe the land will be a winter wonderland as the Earth continues its revolution around the sun, making for ideal snowy conditions in the park for lots of snowshoeing and cross-country skiing!

But I am getting ahead of myself. I plan on thoroughly enjoying this change from summer to fall—warm, gentle days, chilly nights, sweater mornings—the season when the land puts on its earthy fall colors. I recall a verse from an old Phil Ochs song I used to play: *Green leaves of summer turn red in the fall / to brown and to yellow they fade. / And then they have to die / trapped within the circle time parade of changes.* Singing this lovely melody in my head only adds to the vanilla sweetness of my morning hike.

## Some Post-Election Thoughts on Climate Change
*November 11, 2016*

I've been reading about how we need to get behind our president-elect so he has a successful presidency. If a successful presidency would be defined as finding common ground to begin healing the divide that so defines our country right now, I'm all for it. I suspect, though, that the president-elect and the team he is gathering to run the country would define a successful presidency primarily as the successful implementation of his campaign promises. One of his defining promises has to do with energy and climate change, based on his belief that global warming is BS, or a hoax started by the Chinese. I can emphatically say that I will never get behind the president-elect on this issue, and I will do all that I can, as one concerned citizen, to see that he is unsuccessful on this issue.

The president-elect and his team can argue all they want that human-caused climate change is not happening, it is a lie, or a conspiracy, it is bad science, or a left-wing invention. But the science is not on their side. As a bumper sticker I once saw said, "Science doesn't care what you believe." According to nearly every climate scientist not in bed with the fossil-fuel industry, climate change is real, it is primarily caused by human activity, especially the burning of fossil fuels, and it is going to be catastrophic for the Earth that all of us share, regardless of political affiliation, race, nationality, gender, sexual orientation, age, religion, or anything else. Scientists also say that there is still time to prevent the worst impacts of global warming, but only if we act now!

The president-elect and company are arguing with physics. You can't argue with physics and win. Increase greenhouse gases in the Earth's atmosphere, and the planet's climate will change. It's the law. It's like arguing about the existence of gravity while holding a bowling ball over your foot. You can argue all you want, but if you let go, it's going to hurt. A lot. Unfortunately, the impacts of denying gravity are so much more immediate than the relatively slower manifestations of increased greenhouse gases.

It is often argued that the current warming is nothing more than a natural cycle. The planet has always had warming and cooling periods. No argument from science on the latter—the Earth's temperature has always changed as carbon dioxide ($CO_2$) levels and other factors change. Currently, $CO_2$ levels are at around 400ppm (parts per million). Using data gathered from tiny air bubbles in ice cores drilled into ancient Antarctica ice fields, $CO_2$ levels have not been this high for at least 800,000 years. Analyses of shells in deep sea sediments take it back much further, to 10-15 million years ago. Yes, somewhere back there, way back there, way before any modern human species walked the planet, $CO_2$ levels were 400ppm. And the Earth showed it—

sea levels 100 feet higher than they are today, little ice anywhere on the planet—it was a very different planet than the one we all live on.

When our Founding Fathers signed the Declaration of Independence, CO2 levels were about 275ppm. At the time of the Civil War, they were around 285ppm. In 1950, they were a bit above 300ppm. Three days after the recent election, they were 403ppm. Why the increase? The science is clear—human activity, mainly the burning of coal, oil and gas.

All those numbers are not liberal think tank numbers, they are scientific data. Have there been variations in the interpretation of them? Sure. That is what science is—looking at phenomena; developing a theory about this or that facet of the phenomena; subjecting the theory to vigorous testing, observation and data gathering; analyzing the outcomes; making a conclusion as to the accuracy of the theory; making adjustments, re-testing; and, eventually, subjecting conclusions to reviews, challenges and insights from other scientists. As the past few decades have gone by since the theory of global warming first hit the mainstream, the theory has been questioned and scrutinized over and over and over. Today, the science is more certain than ever: global warming is happening, and we are causing it.

Consider this: Say my young child comes down with what appears to be a serious malady, and I take her to 25 doctors and receive 25 medical opinions. Twenty-four doctors tell me she has a serious condition that needs to be acted on immediately, while one doctor says that what appears to be a malady is natural and nothing to be concerned about. What would you think of me if I ignored the 24 doctors who expressed grave concern and instead went with the opinion of the one doctor who is not at all concerned? Not very well, I suspect. Negligence would be an appropriate word. Child abuse, you might say. Well, that is exactly what the president-elect and all other climate-change-deniers are doing about the planet we all live on—ignoring the 97% of scientists that agree that the planet is in trouble.

Fifteen years ago, the Bush administration cut funding for global warming research and systematically sought to suppress and distort the findings of climate scientists. Today, the president-elect wants to do much the same, including eliminating, or significantly reducing, the Environmental Protection Agency. And it looks like he's got Congress behind him on this. These actions are equivalent to removing the mechanisms that monitor your car's oil levels and engine temperature. Of course, none of us want to see the oil or temperature lights come on when we are driving, but what's the alternative? Not knowing something is wrong until your engine is ruined? At least you can buy another car—we can't buy another planet. Such actions and policies are not science-based, and they are not people-based, they are based primarily on the corporate interests of the fossil fuel industry.

Four hundred years ago, Galileo was persecuted for publishing his evidence that supported the Copernican theory that the Earth revolves around the Sun. At a time when the prevailing view was that that the Earth was the center of the Universe, strongly supported by the powerful Catholic Church, Galileo was tried, convicted and sentenced to house arrest for the rest of his life. All for studying and concluding what we now know to be indisputably true—the Earth revolves around the Sun.

Fast forward to our time. Michael E. Mann, Distinguished Professor of Atmospheric Science at Penn State, is a modern-day Galileo. His research into global warming, and his strong confirmation of the link between fossil-fuel emissions and global warming, led to a massive misinformation campaign initiated by the powerful fossil fuel industry. In Mann's own words:

> I set myself up for a completely different life ... I was vilified ... I was called a fraud. I was being attacked by Congressmen. I had death threats, which were actionable enough that the FBI had to come to my office to look at an envelope that had white powder [in it]. I've had threats made against my family. These folks know they don't have to win a legitimate scientific debate. They just need to divide the public. All of that hatred and fear is organized and funded by just a few players. Fossil fuel interests ... finance a very large echo chamber of climate change denialism. They find people with very impressive looking credentials who are willing to sell those credentials to fossil fuel interests. Front groups funded by corporate interests.

Sadly, this campaign, echoed by politicians, conservative talk show hosts, and others, has been very effective—despite the solidity of the science, a significant percentage of Americans still do not believe in global warming. And fossil fuels continue to be mined and piped and burned, and atmospheric $CO_2$ levels continue to rise.

I have dedicated much of my life to providing opportunities for people, especially young people, to experience the wonders of Nature. I do this work because it is so good for children in so many ways to spend time in Nature (it is good for adults too). And I do it because these young people, if they have first-hand experiences in Nature, are more likely to grow up into adult citizens who advocate for the natural world. I love this planet, this amazing little blue ball floating in space. I want others to love it too. From all that I've heard said by the president-elect and the people he is surrounding himself with about their plans, it makes me feel like my work may soon be taking place in a small room on the Titanic. It's a nice room, but what does it matter if the ship is going to sink! This is unacceptable to me.

So, am I a whiner, a sore loser, a doomsayer... if I want to see the president-elect fail in implementing his policies that will so terribly impact the planet we all live on? If I am anything, I am simply a very concerned American citizen that wants to see my government implement environmental policies based on science—good, solid science.

Because without a hospitable planet, no lives matter.

## My Breathing Space
*December 6, 2016*

> *"Perhaps that is what parks are—breathing spaces for a*
> *society that increasingly holds its breath."*
> *~ Terry Tempest Williams*

Yesterday's warm winds have been replaced by a blast of Arctic air—bone-chilling cold, increasingly grey skies, and a stillness that is permeating more and more of me with each breath that I take. I am sitting in one of my sitting spots that I have throughout the park. I've been coming to these spots—to write, reflect, contemplate, or just be—for decades. I haven't been to this one on the Northridge Trail in quite a while.

Knowing it would be cold, I brought along a thermos of hot tea. I figure the tea will assist the early December sun, now and then weakly working its way through the cloud cover, in keeping me warm enough to sit here for a while to take in this dry winter landscape. A flicker flies by; I hear its wings cutting through the crisp December air. I pause and look out at the cold hard granite that makes up the east side of Devil's Canyon. That flicker is sticking around, squawking every now and then. That is the only sound I hear except for the pen moving across the page of my journal.

American naturalist John Burroughs wrote, "If you were to sit under an oak tree for an entire day, you would have enough information to write an entire book." Well, I am not under but next to an oak—a scraggy Gambel oak with a few brown leaves clinging to its dark skeleton-like branches. Except for the green of the conifers, various shades of brown are the dominant colors out here. The color white, which one would expect to see a fair share of this time of year, is conspicuously absent. We've just been through the driest three-month stretch of September through November in at least the last four decades. December is about to grind into its second week and we've yet to see the first measurable snow—a record for latest measurable snow. I suppose this record dry-spell would be a part of the book I could write if I sat here all day.

I hear the rustling of some leaves coming from down the hill in front of me. It sounds like a spotted towhee is looking for something in the duff. I don't see the bird itself, but that sound is typical of the pretty, red-eyed bird that calls this park home year-round.

My back is leaning against the grey remains of a fallen tree that hasn't been alive in a long time. I know this tree; it's been on this hillside for as long as I've been coming here. It reached a height of about 30 feet before it quit growing. It's hard to say for sure, but considering the spacing and placement of the stubs that were its branches, as well as this particular habitat, I'd say it is—or was—a white fir. Based on my estimated calculations—it's been lying on this hillside for thirty years, it stood dead for ten, and it was fifty years old when it died—this weathered backrest started growing ninety years ago. In 1926, just six years after this square mile of land became Pueblo Mountain Park, this tree that is now slowly decomposing was a small young seedling. Through its years, it watched the park's trails being built, it listened to the sounds of the workers who installed the railing at Lookout Point, which sits just across the drainage, it witnessed countless generations of birds and deer and bear come and go. Talk about having enough information to write an entire book!

I suspect Burroughs wrote that little quip about sitting under an oak tree on a nice, warm summer's day. In spite of the hot tea and the weak sun that has disappeared, I've about reached my limit for how long I can sit here and write. The cold Arctic air has now joined the stillness that is permeating my body. As I put the thermos and journal in my pack, I see that the thickening clouds look like they just might bring some snow. That sure would be nice.

## Be Here Now
*February 28, 2017*

It is snowing. It is finally snowing! I stepped out my door an hour ago just as this little storm seemed to be tapering off. Over the course of the couple of miles I have since hiked, I concluded that the storm is not quite done yet. A few minutes of snowfall interspersed with a handful of snowless minutes repeated itself several times during that hour. Weak sunshine has lingered through most of it, strengthening as the snowfall diminished.

I worked my way along the park roads, some sections covered in a couple inches of fresh wet snow, other sections snow-free. The tread of the Tower Trail I am now hiking on is no different. I am searching for a relatively protected place to sit and put some of these thoughts into my journal. Now heading down the Mace Trail, I see a large Douglas fir that looks like it will work just fine as a place to sit and write.

I am mesmerized by watching the falling snow, now coming down fast and hard against a backdrop of ponderosa pines, white firs, and one large Rocky Mountain juniper. It is completely silent—no birds, no snow hitting my jacket, no sound at all. Or is there? As my ears adjust, I believe I can hear a barely perceptible *hiss* coming from all around me. Yes, the falling snow is filling the air with this most subtle sound as it lands on the trees, the shrubs and the ground. Snow music!

It may be snowing now, but there has been very little of it this winter. Many times over the past weeks I have thought to myself that this seems to be the winter that isn't. Instead of snow, it's been very warm and very windy—very unwinter-like. Today's couple of inches of new snow brings the snow season's total to just over 24 inches. It will take another eight feet to bring us to an average winter's snowfall. "I know March and April can be very snowy, and weather patterns do change, so you never know," I keep telling myself. Then I think of last fall's two nearby wildfires, the Beulah Hill Fire and the Junkins Fire, and the *what-ifs* begin.

A handful of minutes pass, and it is now barely snowing. Just a few small flakes are lazily drifting out of the sky. I take a deep breath and can feel the peace of this place fill me. There is no denying that the *what-ifs* associated with the drought we are in could be catastrophic. Not to mention the potential flood damage and destruction that will happen if a strong thunderstorm passes over the 24,000 acres that burned last fall. But there is also no denying that right now, at this moment, in this place, these woods are soaking up a wet snowfall, there is no crazy-strong wind, and there is no wildfire.

After many recent conversations and thoughts and concerns about how dry it is and all that could come out of this dryness, it feels *so good* to let all of that go and simply be here now. To lean into what is at this very moment, in this very spot. To realize that last fall's fires are over, and they are now only thoughts. And all the *what-ifs* are also only thoughts. Right here, right now, is all that is real for me at this moment in time. There is an appropriate time to reflect on what's already done and what might be. Now is not that time.

The snow has stopped. The flutter of a bird's wings nearby and the *peep* of a distant Townsend's solitaire have replaced the snow music. The birds, the snow-covered trees, the cool moist air—these are my only reality at this moment. I will leave thinking about all the rest for another time.

## A Devil of a Trail
*May 30, 2017*

The banter of four happy hikers, unaware of my presence in a sunny spot a short distance off the trail, fades into the forest as they disappear up the trail. I am left with only the sounds of the morning woods—a few buzzing insects and a chorus of bird song. Ovenbird, broad-tailed hummingbird, Steller's jay, dark-eyed junco, black-headed grosbeak, mourning dove, to name a few. The Devil's Canyon Trail is the park's most heavily used trail, and its name is also one of the most commonly used names for American places.

There is Devil's Tower in Wyoming, our nation's first National Monument (designated by Teddy Roosevelt in 1906), which I've read likely got its name due to the misinterpretation of one of its Native names. There's Devil's Sinkhole in Texas, home to a large colony of Mexican free-tailed bats. Then there's the Dirty Devil River in Utah, a place where Butch Cassidy reportedly hid out. Speaking of Utah, I just spent a night at Devil's Canyon Campground near Blanding, named after a nearby canyon that got its devilish name because of the challenges it posed to early settlers. And Devil's Cornfield in Death Valley National Park in California, named after a weed that thrives there; another Devil's Canyon in Utah, that one in the San Rafael Swell; Devil's Peak in Oregon, and the nearby monolith called Devil's Tooth; and Devil's Elbow, a bend in Missouri's Big Piney River that easily floods. There's the popular Devil's Nose, which, among many others, is the name of a mountain ridge in West Virginia *and* a small community in Kentucky. Moving into more distant Americas, Devil's Nose is also part of a hairy train ride in the Andes Mountains in Ecuador. But, I diverge. Back to the Mountain Park's very own Devil's Canyon.

Yes, the Devil's Canyon Trail does see its fair share of hikers. I walked by the trailhead yesterday, a busy, early-summer holiday weekend and counted eleven parked cars. The trail may also be the park's wildest. My definition of *wild* in this instance does not necessarily mean a lack of people, at least on the occasional busy weekend. By wild, I mean self-willed, impermanent, self-organizing, creating its own sense of order. Or, as the frenzied power of lots of moving water can create, its own sense of disorder.

For the forty years I've been hiking this trail, and for half that many that I've been involved in maintaining it, it is clear to me that the Devil's Canyon drainage doesn't give a hoot about the little old trail that winds along its wooded, and occasionally soggy, contours. The seasonal creek that runs through the drainage, known as Devil's Dribble, usually does just as its name implies—it dribbles along, usually hidden beneath rock and soil, occasionally surfacing here and there. It makes its presence more known during the spring runoff, when melting snow increases the flow. But mostly, it just dribbles. Then, every few years, a major rain event serves as a stark reminder that Nature still rules here, and Devil's Canyon can still be a very wild place.

The big rains of early May were the most recent of these disordering events, sending a raging torrent of wild water through the drainage, once again illustrating that any "improvements" done to keep a walkable trail through it are, indeed, impermanent. Massive boulders, huge logs, enormous amounts of soil, branches, rocks and other debris were all moved and thrown about by the self-willed flood that crashed through the Devil's Canyon drainage a few weeks ago. Talk about disorder—at least, by those of us who maintain the trail.

So, we will soon be back out here, again, trying to impose our own sense of order to make the Devil's Canyon Trail a bit more accommodating to the average hiker. But the work will be carried out knowing full well that this is, ultimately, a wild place. Devil's Canyon remains a place where humans are still only visitors, a place where Nature still goes about its business with no regard for the little trail that we are constantly trying to keep up. That is perfectly fine with me!

## Reading the Landscape Calendar
*August 29, 2017*

I recently learned that a tool to help you interpret the meaning of a dream is to give the dream a title. What would an appropriate title be that would capture the primary theme of the dream, or the feeling the dream leaves you with? If I were to utilize that same technique to capture the essence of a hike, the title of this evening's hike would be *Summer is Slipping Away*.

Earlier, I had originally planned to do an afternoon hike, but late summer is still summer, and this afternoon was just too hot for my tastes to be on the trail. So, with the dinner dishes drying in the dish drainer (I still do the dishes the old-fashioned way, with my hands), and the cooling of this late summer evening already underway, here I am on the Mace Trail, sauntering through a landscape with a multitude of hints that fall is fast approaching.

I read somewhere that Thoreau said that if he were plopped down in his Walden woods with no knowledge of the date, he would be able to tell the date within just a day or two by what was happening on the land. Well, I am no Thoreau, and I already know the date, but if I didn't, I think I could get pretty close, maybe a week or so, to the date.

First, the obvious—the warm temps, the place on the horizon where the sun is setting, no snow or signs of it on the ground, the deciduous plants in full leaf—these provide a good sense of the general season. It is clearly not winter, or early spring, or late fall. The oaks and mountain mahogany leaves are still green—so the shorter days of fall that slow down and eventually stop the production of chlorophyll and let the yellows, reds, and oranges show through have not yet arrived. I can see that the leaves lack that new-leaf luster—they are green, but a tired, less vibrant green. That tells me they've been hanging around awhile. I did notice some yellow and a bit of red in the poison ivy patches down along the roads. *Toxicodendron rydbergii* has always been the first plant to show fall colors around here, usually well before the autumn equinox, so these are all helpful indicators of where we are on the calendar.

The wildflowers speak volumes. I see no spring beauty, penstemon, bladderpod, aspen daisy, wild rose, dogbane, or chiming bell in bloom, to name a few spring or early summer flowers. Well, during dry years, these species may not produce blossoms, even if it were May or June. So, their absence can be misleading.

What is in bloom is much more definitive. Around mid-summer, lots of the low-growing hairy golden aster usually start to bring much yellow to the landscape, along with the taller purples of smooth aster. I am seeing lots of both. But the presence of pale goldenrod, and the prolific showing of sunspots and ragleaf bahia—all in yellow daisy bloom—are strong indicators that it is somewhat past mid-summer. I have been seeing some porter aster—white rays around yellow disks—which speak loudly that summer is certainly winding down and fall cannot be too far off. As does tansy aster, which is similar to smooth aster in color with purple or pink rays around a yellow disk, but the curving phyllaries (the bracts that form the cup-like receptacle that sunflower family flower heads sit in) differentiate it from its taller aster cousin.

I pause along the side of the trail and take in the soundscape. Hardly a sound. No birdsong at all, and nary a bird call either. If this were spring or earlier in the summer, there would be much more birdsong associated with the breeding that takes place then.

Put all these clues together, and it points rather convincingly that it is late summer. Not yet fall, but fall is not far off. The fact that the sun has already slipped below the western ridge, the clouds are peachy pink and quickly becoming bluish grey, and it is not quite 7:30, would further help me narrow down the date if I didn't already know it is August 29.

Summer, and this late summer day, are both slipping away. The cool of an almost-fall evening is sending me down the trail, past the just-starting-to-turn poison ivy, back to my home and kitchen where my dishes are now dry and ready to be put away.

## Living in the In-Between

*Summer 2017*

I am living in the *in-between*. Last October, a major wind-driven wildfire raced through a part of my small southern Colorado community. Beulah's several hundred households were evacuated. Eight families lost their homes. Just days after that fire was contained, another windstorm knocked over an electrical transformer, igniting a second major wildfire. The 19,000-acre burn threatened, but ultimately missed my town. These two fires were a repeat of a fire a decade ago, the Mason Gulch Fire, when all of Beulah was evacuated as the fire was making a beeline for town. A shift in the winds saved the day, and the town. We all got to return to our homes, untouched, but warned. This past October, the pattern, and the warning, repeated itself—for most of us, anyway. For those that lost their homes, it was more than a warning.

The months leading up to October's fires were dry, after a string of mostly drier than average years. The few months since have been as dry as any winter I've seen in the forty plus years I've lived in this foothills town in what are called, ironically, the Wet Mountains. Not only drier, but warmer. It used to be that we could count on at least a couple of cold spells each winter of temps well below zero, when cars wouldn't start, pipes froze, and the woodstove cranked hard day and night. Getting much below zero is now a rarity. Not that long ago summers never saw temps get above ninety. The thermometer now flirts with 100F here every summer.

I live in a little cabin on a couple acres of Gambel oak and ponderosa pine (well mitigated, I might add), that has dodged the wildfire bullet several times. Now it feels like I am living in the in-between, between fires that almost swept through my property and the next fire that just might reach it. Saying *if it will happen* no longer seems as accurate as saying *when it will happen.*

That isn't the only in-between I feel I am living in. The wildfire threat is one manifestation, one that I am up-close and personal with, of global climate change. Bill McKibben's 1989 prophetic book *The End of Nature*, which I read shortly after it was first published, first sounded the alarm about global warming to the general public. It was hoped that by making us aware of the catastrophic outcomes of staying on the fossil-fuel path, we would change our ways and keep greenhouse gas levels from increasing to dangerous levels.

And now, here I am, as we all are, somewhere in-between being made aware of the dangers of global warming and doing enough to actually stop the dangerous accumulation of atmospheric greenhouse gases. It's like being on a train and finding out that it is a runaway train, heading for a cliff. We know we are on the train, we know a cliff is somewhere ahead and getting closer, but we can't seem to get the engineer to stop the train. Knowing the train needs to slow down and change course, it seems crazy that the actions and statements of the powers that be—politicians, fossil fuel industry think-tanks and corporations, too many others—seem intent on business-as-usual, and even pushing for the train we are all on to increase its speed.

My sense of living in the in-between has always been accompanied by an estimation of just where I am in the in-between. Am I closer to the start, with lots of miles ahead, am I about halfway, or am I nearing the end? Climate scientists agree that the maximum safe level of $CO_2$ in the atmosphere is 350ppm, a level that will limit global warming to a degree that will not destabilize the climate. Today's atmospheric $CO_2$ levels are 406ppm. This numeric fact, along with the close calls my little community has had with wildfires, further support my sense that I am—we all are—well beyond the halfway point of the climate change in-between. The refrain of a sad, but hopefully not prophetic James Taylor song entitled *Gaia*, comes to mind: *Someone's got to stop us now / Save us from us Gaia / No one's gonna stop us now.*

Maybe this in-between is not between learning about global warming and changing our ways to stop it. Maybe we are between learning of it and actually experiencing catastrophic planetary climate change. (Truth be told, so many of us on the planet have already experienced a climate change catastrophe.) Could it be that the train is not going to change course before it reaches the cliff? Could it be that we just won't stop it in time?

**Afterword**
*February 9, 2023*

Nearly six years have come—and they have gone—since I wrote the final essay in this book. Here are some closing thoughts, a snapshot of this mid-winter day:

I just returned from a brisk afternoon walk in the Mountain Park and was in awe of the sublime beauty that the season's first shovel-worthy snow brought to the park. It's been quite a while since the trees, the fields—the landscape—were graced with a covering of fresh powder, as the few snows we've received so far this season have been the trace-to-an-inch-or-two variety. I am confident this is the driest start to winter the area has ever seen. Last night's eight inches is most welcome, but this eastern front of Colorado's southern foothills remains firmly in drought—even while the rest of Colorado has seen quite a healthy amount of snow so far this winter. Hopefully last night's snow will begin a snowier stretch—we certainly could use the moisture.

The park was quiet today, as there was not a whole lot going on in it. That was not the case the last two days, when Earthkeeper Nature School's happy and eager young students were busily immersed in the school's ideal outdoor classroom. The Mountain Park has been home to this Forest Preschool and Kindergarten since 2018, when Earthkeeper Nature School began operating. It warms my heart to see and hear these little ones in their outdoor classroom filled not with desks and fluorescent lights, but with trees and birds and all things Nature.

I've heard that there has been some serious talk about protecting Pueblo Mountain Park through a conservation easement. It's early in the process, but I am very pleased to learn that the park that taught me so much about Nature, and about starting and building a nonprofit Nature education center, may one day be permanently protected from McMansions and other development, and remain the ideal place where Nature and people intermingle.

The megadrought continues in the western United States. Lake Powell is at 25% of full pool—it was 33% when I wrote about it in a 2005 essay. Scientists just warned that the Great Salt Lake in Utah will be completely dry in five years if current trends continue. It is summer in the Southern Hemisphere, where Chile is experiencing its own megadrought and devastating wildfires.

Climate scientists have been saying for decades that a warmer planet will result in more frequent and intense extreme weather events. The scientists were spot on, as devastating weather events are becoming more and more common. Last month's torrential rains and flooding in California, last summer's deadly record-breaking heat waves in Europe, massive summer flooding in Pakistan from the combination of unusually heavy monsoon rains and heatwave-induced glacial melting—the list gets longer and longer each year as these events occur on every continent.

The Earth's atmospheric CO2 level today is 420ppm. Climate change is increasingly being referred to as the climate crisis. The population of humans just passed eight billion—it was six billion when MPEC was formed 25 years ago. The changing climate and a burgeoning human population have combined to exacerbate the biodiversity crisis—which is often called the Earth's sixth mass extinction. The UN's Environment Program Director Inger Andersen was unequivocal: "...we are at war with nature."

What does the future hold for Pueblo Mountain Park, the classroom of Earthkeeper Nature School, the efforts to protect it from becoming a gated community, the wildflowers and ponderosa pines, the bobcats and bears and birds that live in it? The future of the Mountain Park, or any park, and the future of all human endeavors, is inseparable from the health of the planet. Humans are a part of, and not apart from, Nature, as educator David Orr put it.

The truth is, Nature is in very deep trouble! As a lover of Nature, I refuse to ignore the very real damage that my species is doing to this beautiful blue planet floating in space. Environmental activist and author Joanna Macy says, "The most radical thing any of us can do at this time is to be fully present to what is happening in the world." There is no denying that my love for the Earth, my awe of its beauty and power and mystery, and my obligation to know what is happening to it, are inseparable from the pain I feel for what the human enterprise is doing to the Earth.

Out of that love and out of that pain come the actions I can take, small and humble as they may be, to contribute to healing the destabilizing damage being done to the Earth's systems that our species is wholly dependent upon. I believe it is the human enterprise, the very systems modern humans have created, that must change if we stand any chance of reversing the damage we have done, and continue to do to the Earth, and to ourselves. I believe that every action an individual, a company, a nonprofit, a community, an organization, or a country takes is either a part of the solution—a step, even a tiny step towards the systems changes so needed, or it is a part of the problem—an action or choice that perpetuates the human-created systems that are so detrimental to the Earth.

With a broken heart full of love *and* full of grief for the natural world, I will continue to walk in awe. I will continue to try to make my actions and choices a part of the healing. Nature is my home, it is my only home, it is our only home. Whatever we do to Nature, we do to ourselves.

## Acknowledgements

Thank you to David Anthony Martin and Middle Creek Publishing for all the good work you are doing for the planet and for being so good to work with in helping me bring *Walking in Awe* into reality.

Many thanks to Mary Jean Porter for editing many of the essays in this book. If any errors or inaccuracies slipped by, they are mine and mine alone.

Many thanks to Thom Roberts for help with the cover image

An abridged version of "People Need Nature" was published as a Guest Column in the *Pueblo Chieftain* in 2008.

A slightly modified version of "Living in the In-Between" was published as a part of the "Writers on the Range" project in *High Country News*, July 2017.

## Bibliography of Referenced Works

The Mountains are Calling; Edward Abbey; *Desert Solitaire*

In Love with Nature; Stephen Jay Gould; *Eight Little Piggies*

Hurry Hurry Hurry—For What?; Wendell Berry; "The Pleasures of Eating" essay published in *What are People For?*

Searching for Spring; Aldo Leopold; *Sand County Almanac*

Patriotism as if the Land Mattered; Richard Nelson; "Patriots for the American Land" essay published in *Patriotism and the American Land*

Finding Comfort in the Changing Seasons; Edna O'Brien; quoted in "Redtree Times" website, https://redtreetimes.com/tag/edna-obrien/

The Happy Return of an American Dipper; John Muir; "The Water Ouzel" essay published in *The Mountains of California*

It's Time to Let Go of the Myth; T.H. Watkins; *Stone Time, Southern Utah: A Portrait & A Meditation*

A Quiet Intimacy with Nature; Lyanda Lynn Haupt; *Pilgrim on the Great Bird Continent*

A Quiet Intimacy with Nature; Barry Lopez; *Arctic Dreams*

Finding Meaning in Beauty; Barry Lopez; "Permafrost's Precarious Beauty" essay published in *National Geographic* magazine, December 2007

I Choose it All; Sharman Apt Russell; "The Adored, Buzzing Around Us" essay published in *Orion* magazine, 2009

It Feels so Good to be Home; Richard Nelson; *The Island Within*

Walking Myself Back Home; Wendell Berry; *The Unforeseen Wilderness*

Taking Stock of My One Precious Life; Henry David Thoreau; "Walking" essay published in *Walden and Other Writings of Henry David Thoreau*

Turning Sixty on a Redrock Wilderness Retreat; Mary Oliver; "The Summer Day" poem published in *House of Light*

Some Post-Election Thoughts on Climate Change; Michael E. Mann; quoted in the "Carbon Brief" found at the website: https://www.carbonbrief.org/7-key-scences-leonardo-dicaprio-climate-film-before-the-flood/

My Breathing Space; Terry Tempest Williams; *The Hour of Land*

# About the Author

Dave Van Manen's love of the natural world began when he was a child in the tiny backyard of his New York City home and the summer woods, beaches and bays on Long Island. His thirst for experiencing and learning about Nature has never waned since he moved to Colorado in the mid-1970s. After a career as a musician as part of the husband-and-wife children's music duo known as The Van Manens, Dave founded and was the long-time Executive Director of the nonprofit Mountain Park Environmental Center. Dave is the recipient of numerous awards and honors, including the Enos Mills Lifetime Achievement Award from the Colorado Alliance for Environmental Education. He has authored many articles and essays, including the book *Plants of Pueblo Mountain Park*, a field guide to the flora of Colorado's southeastern mountains. Among Dave's many current projects and enterprises is his work as a nonprofit, green leadership and Nature education consultant through Mountain Coaching and Consulting LLC. He lives with his wife Helene in their cabin in the small town of Beulah in Colorado's southern foothills, where they raised their two children, hiked with their two grandchildren, and has been home base for nearly fifty years.

He is an enthusiastic hiker and backpacker, is rather new to the world of gravel and mountain biking, regularly practices yoga, grows organic veggies in his dome greenhouse, loves to make music, is becoming a better birder, and can often be found hiking trails wherever he may be. **davevanmanen.com**

## About the Illustrator

A love for art has always been an integral part of Scarlett Stulb's life. Born in Pueblo, Colorado, she grew up surrounded by family who supported this love, including her grandfather, Dave Van Manen. Scarlett's passion for creating art has been a guiding light in her life. She has always been ambitious in her career and personal life, graduating with an Associate of Art degree at age 17. Scarlett understands that Illustration and Design can be a vehicle for connecting with the natural world, as well as creating a sense of magic and fantasy. She currently resides in Colorado Springs, Colorado, where she is constantly creating new works, and continually striving to share the joy that creating art gives to her with other people. **linktr.ee/stulbdesign**

## About Middle Creek Publishing

MIDDLE CREEK PUBLISHING believes that responding to the world through art & literature—and sharing that response—is a vital part of being an artist.

MIDDLE CREEK PUBLISHING is a company seeking to make the world a better place through both the means and ends of publishing. We are publishers of quality literature in any genre from authors and artists, both seasoned and as-yet undervalued, with a great interest in works which may be considered to be, illuminate or embody any aspect of contemplative Human Ecology; defined as the relationship between humans and their natural, social, and built environments.

MIDDLE CREEK PUBLISHING's identification as a Human Ecology press is meant to clarify an aspect of the quality in the works we consider for publication, and is meant as a guide to those considering submitting work to us. Our interest is in publishing works illuminating the Human experience of connection to each other, our selves, and to the world we share—to include not only the natural environments, but those that are human constructs such as history, economics, and the social sphere as well—through words, art, story, poetry so that we may reconnect to our potential deeply and more consciously.

Made in the USA
Monee, IL
07 July 2023

38559805R00177